THE HOLY SPIRIT AND YOU Supplement

THE
HOLY SPIRIT
AND YOU
Supplement

A Study Guide To The Spirit-Filled Life
ADAPTED FOR GROUP OR PERSONAL USE

Dennis & Rita Bennett

Bridge-Logos *Publishers*

Gainesville, Florida 32614 USA

Scriptures are quoted from the King James version of the Bible unless otherwise indicated.

HOLY SPIRIT AND YOU SUPPLEMENT
Copyright © 1973 by Bridge-Logos Publishers
Reprinted 2000
All rights reserved.
Library of Congress Catalog Card Number: 73-75963
International Standard Book Number: 0-88270-031-6

Bridge-Logos *Publishers*
PO Box 141630
Gainesville, FL 32614
http://www.bridgelogos.com

INTRODUCTION

The Holy Spirit and You is being used as a textbook in Christian groups of widely differing backgrounds. There have been a number of requests for a study manual to accompany the book, and here it is. We trust it will be a help.

A list of home-study questions is provided for each chapter. Read the chapter first, then complete the questions before the class. Read over the group-study questions as preparation for taking part in small-group discussion. We are not trying to get you to parrot answers out of the book, but to stimulate you to think about the topic and go to the Scripture yourself to "see if these things are so."[1]

---

[1]When we meet to read from Scripture together, what version shall we use? Have you had the experience, as we have, of being with a group of Christians trying to read from the Bible together, and finding that everyone had a different translation? If we are to choose one version on which we can meet together for corporate Bible reading and study, surely the King James is still the one to use, since it has been "The Bible" for so many, many years. From this center, then, each of us can share from our own favorite versions and interpretations, to throw light on the common reading.

Just a comment on the Apocrypha. Some of the students may have Roman Catholic Bibles, and may be puzzled by "extra" books they find that are not in other Bibles. These are the books of the Apocrypha. Most Protestant Bibles don't include them. In Anglican (Episcopalian) Bibles, they are in a separate Those who are to take part in the classes should be registered *before* the first session, and equipped with textbook *The Holy Spirit and You* and this study manual, so that they can come to the first meeting prepared. Those who attend the session without advance preparation should be made to feel welcome but should be asked not to take part in the discussion. This will prevent much wasted time, extraneous questions, and increase respect for the whole procedure. Enforce this kindly but firmly!

The large group session opens with a brief prayer which we have provided for you as a suggested starter. The group leader may use this prayer, and then additional prayer of his own. A Scripture reading follows, then a commentary on the chapter. The leader may want to add more to this commentary from fresh inspiration received during his own preparation. Feel free! This part of the meeting ends with an appreciable period of prayer and praise. Feel free to use your own favorites, of course. The length of this opening time depends on the freedom in the group and the guidance of the Holy Spirit. Do remember that we are talking about the Holy Spirit, and that we should expect His power and freedom to be manifested among us. Praise frees people and makes them more open to give and receive God's blessings. The gifts of the Spirit should be welcomed—if properly ministered, of course. The leader should have had experience in leading charismatic prayer and praise meetings.

Small-group discussion follows, using the questions for group study. These small groups ideally should not contain more than ten persons, and should stay the same from week to week, except that some reassignment will undoubtedly be necessary

section between the Old and New Testaments, and in Roman Catholic Bibles, they are included as part of the Old Testament. The Roman church gives these books equal value with the rest of Scripture. Most Protestants do not accept them at all. Anglicans (Episcopalians) say that they are to be read "for example of life and instruction of manners," but are "not to be applied to establish any doctrine" (Article of Religion VI, *The Book of Common Prayer). You will* enjoy reading these books—they contain much inspiration and blessing. (See *Nine O'Clock in the Morning*, fn. p. 64.)

Please read pp. 205-6 in *The Holy Spirit and You* for further comments on Bible versions, and Bible study.

as the whole project "settles in." Each small group should have a leader.

A "scribe" selected from the group will record interesting insights. The leaders should be appointed by the general leader before the first session, and should meet with the general leader beforehand. The small-group leader's main task is to get everyone to take part. He or she will lovingly control the "eager beavers" who may dominate the discussion (they are very much needed as "spark plugs," provided they will also give the others a chance), and try to encourage the shyer ones to participate. It might be well for the leader to give a little instruction about this at the outset, asking the whole group to help in getting everyone to take part.

After the small group discussions, the whole group should reconvene to share the insights that have come out of the smaller meetings. Also, a series of thirty-minute cassette tape recordings, in which the Bennetts themselves discuss the material chapter by chapter, is available by writing to Box 576, Edmonds, WA 98020. These may be used as part of the teaching time, and will also be useful to the leaders for preparation.

Two and one-half hours should be scheduled for the whole session. The opening should take about thirty minutes; the small groups forty-five minutes to an hour, and the closing about forty-five minutes to an hour. Watch out for time-wasting! It is a temptation to sit and chat, waiting for latecomers. Don't do it! Get started promptly, right on the minute. The others will soon learn to be prompt if they find they have missed something, but if you wait for them, you'll wait every time! The session should end right on the promised time, too, so that people with other obligations can fulfill them.

The leader should remind the group to use the "practical application" given at the end of each chapter. A question relating to this practical application is included at the end of each chapter's small-group discussion questions, except the first chapter.

If the group is unable to plan a full eighteen sessions at one stretch, it might be well to divide the study up into three parts, which could be dealt with at different times of the year. This is the reason for the three "sections": I—Chapters 1-5; II—Chapters 6-13 ; and III—Chapters 14-18.

Note that although this manual is designed mainly with group study in mind, it can, with a little adaptation, be effectively used by a person working alone, or two or three studying together. For such use, we strongly recommend the cassette tapes mentioned above.

May God inspire and bless you as you prepare yourselves to help others.

In Jesus' love,

Dennis and Rita Bennett

CONTENTS

Introduction

SECTION I

SECTION II

SECTION III

SECTION 1 / SESSION 1

CHAPTER 1

THE FIRST STEP

What does it mean to be a Christian? There are so many people who are "nominally" Christian—that is, literally, they are "Christians in name only." Perhaps Western civilization, so-called Christian civilization, is the most difficult of all mission fields—and this field is right under our noses! The "church" people, and those who have been turned off by church, are the most difficult to lead to the reality of Jesus Christ. How very many today think of Christianity as a system of morals, a legalism, or a system of salvation through specified actions and intellectual beliefs! We need to know that

Christians are not people who have accepted a philosophy of life, a way of thinking, a set of rules or principles, but people with God living in them, because they have received Jesus Christ.

You need to know how to share this all-important truth. You need to understand what it means to repent, to be converted, to be forgiven, to be born again, to be a "new creation," not just in your own experience, but to know how to lead others to the same new life in God through Jesus Christ. You need to be able to bear witness to the living Jesus in your life, and you need to be able to tell someone else simply how to receive Jesus.

Questions for Your Home Study

Read chapter one and answer the following questions before your next class. Also prepare to discuss the smallgroup questions.

1. Often the first step in coming to God takes place when Jesus meets an _____ in the person's life.

2. Write the various meanings of the Greek Word *sozo* using your own wording as much as possible.
    _____
    _____

3. What is a Christian? Define. _____
    _____

4. What other terms mean the same thing as "salvation"? Give at least four. Can you think of others besides those given in the book? _____

_____

_____

_____

5. What part of a believer has been reborn? _____

_____

6. a. Name the three parts of a human being. _____

_____

   b. Where is this in the Bible? _____

7. At what point does the Holy Spirit come to live in a human being? _____

_____

8. When does eternal life begin? _____

_____

9. Give four steps in accepting forgiveness and receiving new life. _____

_____

10. In addition to sharing your personal testimony, do you have at your fingertips a "Plan of Salvation" to help you in witnessing? (Turn to page 154 in *"The Holy Spirit and You"* . . .) and read the second and third paragraphs for further help.) _____

_____

11. Write a simple prayer of your own, such as you might use in leading someone to Jesus Christ.

_____

_____

_____

Large-Group Meeting

Leader opens with prayer:

Dear Heavenly Father, help me to be a willing and effective witness to lead many people into Your kingdom. As I confess Your Son Jesus among men, I rejoice to know that He confesses me before Your throne. May Divine love so flow through me that I may be a channel of Your healing, saving love. In Jesus' name, I pray. Amen.

Scripture

"Whosoever therefore shall confess me before men, him will I confess also before my Father which is in heaven." (Matt. 10 :32) .

----

[2]The chorus book Renewal in Song is no longer available. Fortunately today there are an abundance of chorus books to choose from

Commentary

The leader will share from the Commentary found at the beginning of the chapter, and add to it as he or she feels led.

Prayer and Praise

The whole group should spend a time of praise and prayer, the length depending on the freedom of the people and the guidance of the Holy Spirit through the group leader. Sing some familiar or easy-to-learn choruses, and also invite special prayer concerns. Some songs you might sing are: . . . "Everybody Ought to Know," 'I'm Singing Wonderful! Wonderful!,' "Therefore With Joy Shall Ye Draw Water," "His Praise Fills the Temple."[2] When learning a new song or chorus, don't be afraid to sing it through several times until people learn it. The value of choruses is that they can be so easily learned.

Small-Group Discussion

1. In the example given in the first chapter, do you think our New England friend did a good job of witnessing? Why, or why not?

2. This was a very simple example of being a witness; what other situations might you get into, and what other resources might you need?

3. In this example, the believer gave only the simplest kind of statement about who Jesus is. Should there

be a follow-up? What suggestions would you make? Do you know how to prove the divinity of Jesus through Scripture? Through experience?

4.   Repentance and forgiveness of sins must come before Jesus can come into our hearts. What does repentance mean? When do you think the neighbor repented?

5.   How can you avoid being mechanical or awkward when using a "Plan of Salvation" to help you witness? What are the advantages of such a method?

6.   What do you think our housewife in the example might have done if her friend had not spontaneously asked Jesus for help?

7.   In one *National Geographic* article about a race of aborigines in the Philippines (August 1972) the author describes the gentleness of this primitive tribe, and then says, "Maybe we ought to look back to primitive peoples to find out where the world went wrong. There seems to be a growing sense that it has gone wrong. Maybe we can learn from the Tasadays."

    What would be your comments on this statement and idea? Has the world "gone wrong"? Would a

---

[3]See notes at the back of this book

return to primitive days solve the problem? Do you
suppose the primitive people were really better?
What does the Bible mean when it says we were
"born in sin"?

8. Many people think it narrow to say "Jesus is the
only way."

   a. How would you answer someone who
   challenged you on the statement that Jesus is
   the only way to God?

   b. What did Jesus Himself say about it? (See John
   16.)

9. Have you ever led a person to Jesus Christ? Tell
us about it.

10. Jesus is a Man, and He is in heaven. How can He
live *in* another human being?

Conclusion

The whole group comes back together and shares
the insights gained in the smaller units. At this time
the cassette tape may be played.[3] The meeting closes
with a further period of prayer and praise. During this
praise time, it is best to sing without books so the Holy
Spirit can move with greater freedom. You will want
to sing some additional choruses that the majority of
the group are already familiar with. The leader may
ask for those who are not sure if they have received
Jesus as Savior to indicate their desire to do so. The

leader should then lead them, and all others in the group who would like to join in, in a prayer asking Jesus into their lives. (See pp. 7 in *The Holy Spirit and You*.)

Practical Application

Look for an opportunity to witness to someone this week. Pray that you will not only witness but be able to help that person receive Jesus Christ.

Write out your own personal plan of witnessing. Mark the verses in the sequence you've chosen in your Bible for easy reference. It's good to have a small Bible for this purpose, one that fits easily into a pocket or pocketbook. For witnessing to a Jewish person, you might work on a plan using the Old Testament Scriptures.

NOTES

SECTION I / SESSION 2

CHAPTER 2

THE OVERFLOW

The experience of Pentecost is not confined to the early days of the Church, but is for all believers today. It is essential that believers not only be *given* the Holy Spirit, which happens at the new birth, but that they *receive* the power which comes with the Baptism in the Holy Spirit. Only thus can we really meet the world's challenge and the world's needs. The Baptism in the Holy Spirit is the *outflow* of the power of God the Holy Spirit from where He dwells within the believer—in the spirit—to inundate, or baptize, the outer man, soul, and body. It is a release of the Spirit. When this takes place, then the Holy Spirit can pour from the believer into the world like "rivers of living water," as Jesus promised (John 7:38).

11

On the Day of Pentecost we read: "And they were all filled with the Holy Ghost." But it didn't stop there. If it had, there would have been no spread of the faith throughout the world; it would have remained confined in the hearts of those first believers. But the record goes on, ". . . and (they) began to speak." They were filled, and then they began to *overflow*.

Questions for Your Home Study

1. Name the three parts of the soul or psyche. ————

   _____

2. Salvation may be called the ——— coming of the Holy Spirit, while the Pentecostal experience may be called the ——— flow of the Holy Spirit.

3. a. What needs to happen in order for the spirit to gain the strongest influence over the soul and the body? ———————————

      _____

   b. Give six names for this experience. ———————

      _____

4. What is the Baptism in the Holy Spirit called in the Episcopalian (Anglican), Roman Catholic, Orthodox, Lutheran, and some other churches?

   _____
   _____

5. What does the word "baptize" really mean? _____
   _____

6. Look up the meaning of the old Jewish feast of
   Pentecost. Do you see any connection between
   this and the Christian's Pentecost? Do some
   research on it. _____
   _____
   _____
   _____

7. How can the Baptism in the Holy Spirit help
   Jesus refresh the world? _____
   _____
   _____

8. In how many of the Gospels is the story told of
   Jesus' receiving the power of the Holy Spirit?
   List the references. _____
   _____
   _____

Large-Group Meeting

Prayer

Father, thank You for giving me Your Holy Spirit
through Your Son Jesus when He came to live in me.
In Jesus' name, please help me to let Your Spirit
empower me to think and act and be more like Jesus.
Amen.

Scripture

"But ye shall receive power, after that the Holy Ghost is come upon you; and ye shall be witnesses unto me both in Jerusalem, and in all Judaea, and in Samaria, and unto the uttermost part of the earth." (Acts 1:8)

Commentary

The leader will share from the Commentary found at the beginning of the chapter, and add to it as he or she feels led.

Prayer and Praise

Suggested songs from *Renewal in Song* are: "I've Got Peace Like a River," "Magnify the Lord With Me," "His Name Is As Ointment Poured Forth." After prayer and praise, break up into small discussion groups.

Small-Group Discussion

1. Why do the writers feel on sound scriptural ground when they use the term "Baptism. in the Holy Spirit"?

2. Why is it important to remember *where* the Holy Spirit resides in the life of the believer? (That is, in the spirit.)

3. Give an example of how you could *get* something and yet not have *received* it. This might be a good

thing to act out in the class. Think up a little skit in which something is given but not received, or in which a person is present but not received.

4. Why is it important for the physical body to receive the outflow of the Spirit?

5. Has the Baptism in the Holy Spirit helped Jesus refresh others through you?

6. Did you witness to someone about Jesus Christ this past week? Were you also able to pray with him or her actually to receive Jesus as Savior and Lord?

Conclusion

Large group resumes for sharing and praise. The tape may be used.[4]

Practical Application

Pray for an opportunity to share about the "overflow" of the Holy Spirit this coming week.

Begin reading through the Gospel of John, and one other Gospel of your choice, looking for the words, "Holy Spirit," "the Spirit," "the Comforter," etc., and mark them. See how often the Holy Spirit is mentioned and what the Scripture tells us about Him.

How many times does Paul refer to the Holy Spirit in the first 16 verses of Romans 8 ? How many can you find?

NOTES

SECTION I / SESSION 3

CHAPTER 3

WHAT DO THE SCRIPTURES SAY?

The Bible is the inspired record of God's dealings with us, and our present experiences with spiritual things must be in line with this record. If you can't find your spiritual experience in the Scripture, it isn't in the mainstream, and if it is spoken *against* in the Scripture, you must renounce it completely! If something is essential to our life in God, it will be clearly told about in the New Testament, and usually foretold in the Old Testament. The experience of receiving the power of the Holy Spirit today passes these tests with flying colors. Study the Scriptures carefully so that you can answer those who question you about it. Remember that we need to know what the Bible as a whole says about a subject, not just what an individual "proof text" may seem to be saying.

Questions for Your Home Study

1. Personal experience is vital and central to our life in God, yet we should not accept an experience that is not clearly supported by: _____

   _____

2. Why was it that the people in Nazareth, and even Jesus' own family, didn't recognize Jesus as the Messiah during the first thirty years of His life?

   _____

3. What event in Jesus' life followed immediately after His empowering with the Holy Spirit? Why? ____

   _____

4. What results in His life followed immediately after His empowering? _____

   _____

5. What three events had to take place before the Holy Spirit could come to dwell in man, before human beings could be born again of the Spirit? (Heb. 9:22, I Cor. 15:17, John 7:39, John 17:1, and Luke 24:26) _____

   _____

6. When was the Holy Spirit given to the first believers? (John 20:1-22) _____

7. When was the Holy Spirit poured out on all flesh?

   _____

8. In addition to the initial outpouring of the power of the Holy Spirit as recorded in Acts 2:4, give four other places in the Book of Acts where the same empowering was experienced: _____

_____

9. Is it necessary to have the laying-on-of-hands in order to receive the Holy Spirit? Give Scripture to support your opinion. _____

_____

10. Find the place in the Book of Hebrews where the writer (some think it to have been Paul) says that one of the six basic principles of the doctrines of Jesus Christ was the "doctrine of baptisms." (Use your concordance.) How many baptisms did Jesus refer to in Acts 1:5? Write down Scripture for three baptisms: _____

_____

Large-Group Meeting

Prayer

Dear Father, I open my inner ears to hear Your Son Jesus speak to me through the inspired pages of Scripture. Increase this hunger in me to read and study the Bible, expecting to be fed with Your abundance. I know as I do this, not only will I be satisfied, but I will be kept in a place of safety. I praise You, Lord, for taking such good care of Your children! In Jesus' name, I pray. Amen.

Scripture

"All scripture is given by inspiration of God, and is profitable for doctrine, for reproof, for correction, for instruction in righteousness; that the man of God may be perfect, thoroughly furnished unto all good works." (II Tim. 3 :16-17)

Commentary

The leader will share from the Commentary found at the beginning of the chapter, and add to it as he or she feels led.

Prayer and Praise

Suggested songs: "Wonderful and Marvelous," (Add the verse: "Soon He's coming back again, O praise His dear name; Yesterday, today, forever, Jesus is the same!"), "A Boundless, Eternal Supply," "Anointed," After prayer and praise, break up for small discussion groups.

Small-Group Discussion

1. When did the Holy Spirit come into Jesus' human life, and how does this compare with our experience? Discuss.

2. Jesus was baptized with water; then the Holy Spirit came upon Him in power. To what does this

empowering correspond in the experience of the individual Christian?

3. a. Discuss the differences between the baptism spoken of in I Cor. 12:13 and that in Luke 3:16.

  b. In each case, who is the Baptizer, and into Whom is the person baptized?

4. Does the Scripture that says God poured out His spirit upon all flesh mean that everyone is automatically saved? Why, or why not?

5. What was Jesus' most important instruction? Give Scripture. What was Jesus' second most important instruction? Give Scripture. What should these instructions lead the baptized-in-the-Spirit Christian to do today?

6. The apostles were called "witnesses of the resurrection," but how can this be, since they did not actually see Jesus rise from the dead?

7. Why is it important to remember that the Holy Spirit was already living in those first disciples of Jesus (John 20) before they were baptized in the Holy Spirit? How was the situation different for the three thousand who believed on the Day of Pentecost?

8. When did the "last days" begin? Are we living in the "last of the last days?" Why, or why not?

9. Some teach that Pentecost only happened once. What Scripture in Acts 11 clearly shows that the experience was repeated?

10. Does the receiving of Jesus as Savior always precede the Baptism with the Holy Spirit? Why?

11. Does baptism with water always precede the Baptism with the Holy Spirit? Give Scripture for your answer.

12. What is the normal order of the three?

13. If you have the chance to witness to a group of people from varying denominations, would it be a good idea to discuss the various modes and doctrines of baptism with water? Should you insist that they follow your own pattern and practice, or that of your church? What would happen, probably, if you did this? Read I Cor. 1:17.

14. Did you have an opportunity to witness to someone this past week about the Baptism with the Holy Spirit (the overflow)? How did you do it? Through a verbal contact, letter, literature, tapes, or other method?

Conclusion

The large group resumes for sharing and praise. The tape may be played.

Practical Application

Are you prepared to show someone the Scriptures in your own Bible on the Baptism in the Holy Spirit? Go through the Gospels and Acts and some of the Epistles and mark your Bible so that you will be able to easily find these passages. You may want to use a colored pencil or some other convenient way of marking. You need a plan to be able to share effective witness about this experience, just as you did with salvation.

NOTES

SECTION 1 / SESSION 4

CHAPTER 4

PREPARING TO RECEIVE THE BAPTISM IN THE HOLY SPIRIT

One of the most dangerous threats to the world today is the revival of the occult. Witchcraft and sorcery are running wild. Also, many people are ensnared in one or another of the cults. You need to know about these things, not only to protect yourself or disentangle yourself from such things, but to help others to get themselves free.

The religion editor of a leading daily newspaper in one of our large cities wrote this statement in his column: "Occultism? The term covers anything having to do with the mysterious or supernatural. Which means Christianity itself is `occult.' " Can you refute this

25

statement? You may be hearing many like it in the days that are coming. Can you clearly distinguish between Christianity and the psychic and occult things that are so popular today?

In addition to making sure that we have cleansed our souls from any involvement with wrong beliefs and teachings such as are found in the cults and in the occult, we also need to be sure that we are ready to allow God to correct and rid us of any attitude or behavior that is displeasing to Him. Examine yourself to see that you have offered to God any known sin in your life. Be sure that you are not hanging on to a "pet" vice, a quirk in your behavior that you and perhaps others think is funny, something which makes you think of yourself as a bit of a "character." An example would be a bad temper. Some say: "I'm shortfused! I've got an Irish temper!" But God doesn't like tempers, Irish or otherwise. Or perhaps you allow yourself the luxury of a little depression and self-pity. Well, be prepared to let go of it! Perhaps you have more serious behavior problems. Today some churches are condoning various kinds of deviant behavior, even saying that such behavior is simply a "way of life." If you have some serious problem, don't feel condemned, for God does not regard one problem differently from another, He just wants to heal them all. Don't try to tell Him that your problem is a "way of life" and a part of your personality, ask Him to heal it. Last but not least, you cannot hang onto resentments and hatred toward people. You must forgive all those who have wronged you, and pray for them, and ask God to give you real love for them.

Questions for Your Home Study

1. What is the first and most important question
    to ask of someone coming to receive the
    Baptism in the Holy Spirit? _____
    _____

2. What is meant by reincarnation? What groups teach
    it? _____
    _____

3. How would you answer someone who said that
    reincarnation was taught in the Bible? _____
    _____
    _____

4   List the main occult or psychic practices. _____
    _____
    _____

5. The writings of what two occult leaders are very
    popular ? _____
    _____

6. Is hypnotism dangerous? Why, or why not? _____
    _____

7. What is spiritism? Spiritualism? _____
    _____

8. Do the disembodied souls or spirits of departed human beings ever revisit the earth? _____

_____

9. What is a cult? Give examples of several cults, and some description of their teachings. _____

_____

_____

10. Comment on the statement: "There are many ways to God." _____

_____

11. What is meant by sorcery? Witchcraft? _____

_____

Large-Group Meeting

Prayer

Lord, we are sorry if we have allowed wrong beliefs or teachings of any kind to lodge in our minds. Help us to be careful of what we read, see, and hear, so that the enemy cannot gain influence in our thinking. We dedicate our thought-life to You. May Your pure mind fill every corner of our own more and more. Dear God, put the searchlight of Your truth upon us, so that we may recognize our needs and come to You for healing. In Jesus' name, we pray. Amen.

Scripture

"If we say that we have fellowship with him, and walk in darkness, we lie, and do not the truth: But if we walk in the light, as he is in the light, we have fellowship one with another, and the blood of Jesus Christ his Son cleanseth us from all sin." (I John 1:6-7)

Commentary

The leader will share from the Commentary found at the beginning of the chapter, and add to it as he or she feels led.

Prayer and Praise

Suggested songs from *Renewal in Song:* "This Is the Year of Jubilee," "In the Name of Jesus," "He Is Lord," Praise God for showing you His truth and protecting you from all erroneous teachings, then break up into small discussion groups.

Small-Group Discussion

1. Is it possible to take "some of the good from all religions" and put it together into one? What very popular modern cult attempts to do this?

2. Is Christianity founded on the ethical teaching of Jesus? Why, or why not?

3. What is the relationship between the cults and the older pagan religions, Buddhism and Hinduism, for

example? Why do you suppose some people today turn to the pagan religions?

4. What is "metaphysics" in the sense it is used by religious seekers? Why is it misleading?

5. What is the difference between astrology and astronomy? Why is astrology wrong? What does the Bible say about it? (Use your concordance. The Bible sometimes speaks of astrologers as stargazers, observers of times, etc.)

6. How is fortune-telling (precognition) different from prophecy? Why is fortune-telling wrong?

7. How do such psychic manifestations as mind-reading and clairvoyance differ from the Holy Spirit's gift of knowledge?

8. When Philip was caught up by the Spirit in Acts 8, was this levitation? Astral projection? Why, or why not?

9. What should you do if you discover that the person who wants you to pray with them to receive the power of the Holy Spirit has been involved in cults or the occult at any time in his or her life?

10. What would you do if they refused your counsel?

11. In what way have you started to mark your Bible to easily locate the Scriptures you will use in building faith for others to receive the power of the Holy Spirit? Did you have an opportunity to share from these Scriptures with someone this week?

Conclusion

Large group resumes for sharing and praise. The tape may be played. The leader might ask those who still have questions and would like to talk further or pray to renounce some specific things to meet him and /or some counselors immediately after the class. For those who can't stay but want this help, he should make private appointments for a later time.

Practical Application

Go through your library and see if you have any books or magazines which teach that the cults or occult are beneficial. Get rid of them in such a way that no one else can be harmed by them. Walk through your house or apartment and dedicate every room to the Lord Jesus. If there is a picture, poster, figurine, etc., that doesn't seem in keeping with your life in Christ, dispose of it. (Discuss this with your mate or children if it is something belonging to them.) In prayer go through the rooms of your life and see if there is some wrong thinking or habit pattern that needs to be brought to Jesus for healing. Write these down and pray about them until you see a change. Thank God for every little bit of progress!

NOTES

SECTION 1 / SESSION 5

CHAPTER 5

HOW TO RECEIVE THE BAPTISM IN THE HOLY SPIRIT

Jesus Christ planned that the complete good news of the Gospel would be announced, and that therefore as each person was brought alive in Him, so the power of the Holy Spirit would be released and each person would be empowered to tell others. Receiving the Baptism in the Spirit is essential if the people you lead to Jesus are going to lead others, and show them how to witness and in turn to bring others. You must know how to pray with people to receive the empowering of the Holy Spirit and *know* that they will receive, and speak in tongues.

Every now and then a Christian will have a wonderful

sense of God's presence with him or her, a joy and peace that is certainly the work of the Holy Spirit. Then it will go away, not to return perhaps for years. This is not the Baptism in the Holy Spirit. The Baptism in the Holy Spirit is not just a one-time experience, a sudden mountaintop that comes and goes without warning.

When we first receive Christ, we often have a dramatic experience, but the most important thing is that we have begun a new life in Jesus, which goes on from day to day. We are living a "saved" life. Jesus saves or rescues us from dangers daily. Salvation began at a particular point in time, but it goes on to become a way of life. So it is with receiving the Holy Spirit. It may begin with a dramatic experience, a Pentecost, but the nature of the Baptism in the Spirit is that it continues day by day. As we live by the power of the Spirit in a new way, our souls and bodies continue to be baptized in the Holy Spirit. Paul says: "Be being filled with Spirit." This is the real translation of Eph. 5:18. Speaking in tongues is not just an outward sign that may or may not accompany a dramatic experience of the Holy Spirit; speaking in tongues is the effective means by which the Holy Spirit moves out into soul and body with new freedom; it is an integral part of Jesus baptizing us in the Holy Spirit, and it is to continue day by day. As we speak in tongues, we enable the Lord Jesus to keep us free in the Holy Spirit.

To lead a person to Christ and not see to it that he is baptized in the Holy Spirit is like giving someone a car, filling it with gasoline, but not showing him how to start it or drive it. When a person receives Jesus, he receives everything he needs to live a full and powerful Christian life, but needs to be shown how to release the power of the Holy Spirit.

Questions for Your Home Study

1. In this empowering of the Holy Spirit, who is the Baptizer? *(Underline the correct answer.)* The Holy Spirit, the Church, Jesus Christ, the minister who prays.

2. When should a person begin to produce the fruit of the Spirit? (See John 15:4-5; I Cor. 6:17.)

    _____

    _____

3. Does it take time for spiritual fruit to grow?   _____

    _____

4. After the Baptism in the Holy Spirit should there be an increase in the fruit of the Spirit?   _____

    _____

5. How did the apostles know *immediately* when a Christian received the Baptism in the Holy Spirit?_____ Give Scripture.

    _____

6. a. Are the emotions necessarily involved in speaking in tongues?_____

    _____

b. Can a person speak in tongues and feel no
emotion whatsoever? _____
_____

7. Does speaking in tongues come from the soul or
the spirit of the Christian? Give Scripture.
_____
_____

8. Why is this important to know?
_____

9. Does the Holy Spirit Himself speak in tongues?
_____

10. Did Jesus speak in tongues? Why, or why not?
_____

11. List the abc's of receiving the Baptism in the Spirit.
a.
b. _____
c. _____

12. Which of the following is correct? (*Underline the*
correct answer.) The Baptism in the Holy Spirit
is: an end in itself, a sign of real spiritual maturity;   the
final blessing God has to give Christians; the beginning
of a new dimension for Christians; a reward.

Large-Group Meeting Prayer

Dear God, our Father, please teach us all that it means
to know Your Son Jesus as our Baptizer. Thank You that

Jesus is always the same and that He's baptizing believers today with the Holy Spirit just as He did nearly two thousand years ago. Father, if we ever needed power to stand strong in our faith, it is today. Thank You that You haven't left us out but have provided for us above all we could ask or think! Praise You, Father, praise You, Jesus Christ, praise You, Holy Spirit. In Jesus' name I pray. Amen.

Scripture

"For every one who asks receives, and he who seeks finds, and to him who knocks it will be opened." (Luke 11:10 RSV) "Jesus Christ the same yesterday, and today, and forever." (Heb. 13:8)

Commentary

The leader will share from the Commentary found at the beginning of the chapter, and add to it as he or she feels led.

Summary

If you want to be effective in helping others receive the Baptism in the Spirit, first help them clear away any intellectual questions blocking them, being sure they are properly prepared, as has been described in the first chapters of the book. Build their faith by showing them what God says about the Baptism in the Holy Spirit in the Scriptures, by giving them your own experience, and then encouraging them to step out in faith and receive. You will find that the next wonderful experience after your own Baptism in the Spirit, is praying with and seeing another receive!

Prayer and Praise

Praise God for the baptism with the Holy Spirit, (whether you have actually received this baptism as yet or not). Worship God and just forget about yourself. Break up into small discussion groups. Suggested songs: "My Redeemer and Saviour Divine," "Sweep Over My Soul," "The Breath of God."

Small-Group Discussion

1.   I Corinthians 14:14-15 gives the only definition in the Scripture for "praying in or with the Spirit."   (In Greek "in" or "with" can be and frequently are used interchangeably. Look at verses 2,4,6,13-16, noting the ins and withs, for example.) Since this definition is equated with praying or speaking in tongues, is it true that Christians who do not speak in tongues do not pray in or with the Spirit? (Answer this in the light of John 4:23-24.)

2.   Is praying in tongues a more Spirit-guided prayer than praying in a known language? Discuss the respective merits of praying in your own language, and praying in tongues. Should we do both? Give Scripture.

3.   What are some other reasons for praying, speaking,

and singing in tongues? Give Scriptures.

4. What happened to Jesus immediately after He had received the Holy Spirit with power?

5. How does this relate to your own life and experience?

6. Do temptations and attacks of the enemy come and go, or continue with intensity? What happened with Jesus?

7. Can darkness remain where the Light is? (Read I John 1:5-7,9.) Discuss.

8. Give some sword-like Scriptures that have helped you deal with the enemy. Share them with the group. Read them aloud.

9. This week did you find any reading material, pictures, posters, etc., in your home which the Holy Spirit led you to get rid of? If it would not be embarrassing to you or someone else in your family, share your experience in this matter.

Conclusion

Large group resumes for sharing and praise. The tape may be used. The leader may ask those who would like to be baptized with the Spirit to stay after the meeting for prayer. He may ask for a show of hands—while heads are bowed in prayer—so that no one will be missed.

Practical Application

If you have received the Baptism in the Spirit, have you ever prayed with another person to receive? (On an individual basis, it is best to pray for a member of your own sex.) If you still are not confident as to how to go about this, talk to one who has been used frequently in this way. Ask if you may accompany them the next time they are requested to pray. If there is a church in your area that is a "spiritual oasis," talk to the pastor and ask if you can train to be a prayer counselor. Look for opportunities; God will provide them if you are ready and willing.

NOTES

SECTION II /SESSION 6

CHAPTER 6

INTRODUCTION TO THE GIFTS
OF THE HOLY SPIRIT

Paul clearly distinguishes between "gifts" of the Holy Spirit, and "fruit" of the Spirit. The gifts are the manifestation of Jesus' power and loving deeds and words through believers, whereas the *fruit is* the *character* of Jesus coming through the believer's life. We are not given spiritual gifts as awards of merit or badges of achievement, nor are they "permanent assignments" to give us status. The gifts, though, are an integral part of the Gospel, and all believers should expect to manifest them. The seven gifts listed first in I Cor. 12, are all to be found in the Old Testament, and in the New Testament before Pentecost. The last two came at Pentecost: tongues and interpretation. God does not withdraw His gifts because they are misused. The gifts are not a sign of holiness or merit, but of faith—not just faith in general, but each gift requires a specific faith to manifest it.

Questions for Your Home Study

1. To whom is a gift of the Holy Spirit given?

_____

2. Are the gifts of the Spirit marks or badges of merit or achievement? Are they "awarded" to people?

_____

_____

3. a. Does every believer have all nine gifts of the Spirit?
   b. Can he or she manifest them just as he or she chooses?

_____

4. When a believer often manifests a particular gift, we may say that he has a

_____ in that gift.

5. List the first seven gifts of the Spirit. Give examples of these in the Old Testament.

_____

_____

6. List the two latest gifts of the Spirit. Give Scripture for these gifts in the New Testament. _____

7. Does Paul list tongues and interpretation last in I Corinthians 12 because they are inferior to the other gifts? (See page 85.)

8. The gifts of the Spirit should be: (underline one) hoped for, tolerated, greatly desired. Why?_____

9. a. What does the word "charismatic" mean?

   b. It is being picked up by secular writers in politics and other fields. How are they using it?

10. Should Christians follow signs?_____

11. Does God give signs to encourage believers today?

Large-Group Meeting

Prayer

Thank You, Father, for the gifts that Your Holy Spirit distributes to us and through us. Help us to covet these gifts, and come behind in none of them, being used in all of them as You inspire and lead. Please keep us from the sin of pride. Keep us aware that the gifts without the fruit of the Spirit, although they still help those to whom we minister, leave *us* as mere noisy gongs. May we always minister in love so that people will see Jesus, and be led to receive Him, and the Baptism in the Holy Spirit. Thank You, Jesus. Amen.

Scripture

"Now concerning spiritual gifts, brethren, I would not have you ignorant." (I Cor. 12 : 1)

Commentary

The leader will share from the Commentary found at the beginning of the chapter and add to it as he or she feels led.

Prayer and Praise

After prayer and praise, break up into small discussion groups. Suggested songs: "I Want More of Jesus," "I'm So Glad I Belong to Jesus," "We Worship and Adore Thee."

This might be a good point to give instruction about raising the hands to praise the Lord. Many erroneously regard this as a kind of "fanatical" gesture. Point out the Scripture: Exod. 17:10-12; I Kings 8:22; I Kings 8:54; Ps. 141:2 ; Neh. 8 :6 ; I Tim. 2 :8. Explain that this is the ancient scriptural gesture of prayer and praise. No one has to pray this way, but encourage them to try it. Explain that it is a freeing gesture to stand with uplifted hands. It is the gesture of surrender, and also of love. Sing a chorus such as "Amazing Grace," and invite the group to lift their hands as they sing it, especially the "last verse" with just the words "Praise God!" repeated throughout.

Small-Group Discussion

1. Why is it unfortunate for believers to desire the fruit of the Spirit without the gifts?

2. If God's gifts are perfect, how is it that they can be misused?

3. Why doesn't God withdraw His gifts if they are misused?

4. If a Christian prays with you to be baptized with the Holy Spirit, and you later discover that he or she was living an immoral life at the time you were prayed with, does that mean that you might have received a wrong spirit?

   Why, or why not?

5. In the past, when people misused the gifts, what has often been the reaction of the pastor? Is this reaction scriptural?

6. What is a constructive action to take if someone ministers the gifts unwisely?

7. This week, did you make any headway in preparing to pray, or actually praying with a person for the Baptism in the Holy Spirit? Tell about it.

Conclusion

Large group resumes for sharing and praise. The tape recording may be used.

Practical Application

Have you ever asked God to release his Gifts through you? Are you willing to be a channel for any of the gifts of the Holy Spirit? If you have any reservations, write them down, and pray about them. If there are no reservations, pray this week (or right now) telling the Lord you are available.

NOTES

SECTION II /SESSION 7

CHAPTER 7

THE GIFTS OF TONGUES AND INTERPRETATION

Many leaders and churches are coming to accept that the various gifts of the Holy Spirit are still at work in the church. Often the last to be accepted is the gift of tongues, with its accompanying gift of interpretation. Such things as wisdom, knowledge, and healing don't require as much explaining. Most people have an idea, although often a mistaken one, as to what *prophecy is.* "Speaking in tongues," however, seems to be more of a mystery, so we need to understand these last two gifts thoroughly ourselves, and be able adequately to explain them to others.

We have already learned about speaking in tongues as a manifestation of the Baptism in the Holy Spirit and as a very important resource in private communication with God, a major means of refreshing the believer by strengthening the influence of the Holy Spirit in his life. Now we go on to study the *gift* of speaking in tongues, which is the use of speaking in tongues as specifically moved by the Holy Spirit in a group or meeting, accompanied by the gift of interpretation.

As people study the Scriptures and apply them to their lives, these gifts of utterance will be the blessing in and to the church they were intended to be. Each gift of God has a purpose, just as each member of the Body has a purpose, and none should be ignored or left out. Unless all the gifts are manifested as God intended, the Body of Christ on earth will be handicapped.

Questions for Your Home Study

1. What are the "three gifts of utterance" and their purposes? _____
    _____
    _____
    _____

2. What are the two basic ways in which speaking in tongues may be used? _____
    _____

3. The gift of tongues, with interpretation, is first of
all a sign to _____
and secondly to build up the _____
_____. Give two Scriptures. _____

4. Give a simple definition for:
speaking in tongues _____
_____
the gift of tongues _____
_____
interpretation of tongues _____
_____

5. What is "singing with the Spirit"? Is it scriptural?
Who may do it? Can it be done privately? In a
group? _____
_____
_____
_____

6. Should every believer bring a gift of tongues in
the same meeting? Give Scripture. _____
_____
_____

7. What was Paul's first reason for remonstrating with
the believers in Corinth? (See I Cor. 1.) How would
this compare with our situation today? _____
_____
_____
_____

8. What were other reasons for correcting the Corinthians? (I Cor. 11 & 14) _____

_____

9. Do you think the charismatic renewal with the manifestations of the Holy Spirit may be an effective tool to reach Jewish people for Jesus?

_____

_____

Large-Group Meeting

Prayer

Father in heaven, we want to be used in any way that will help to bring people to You and will build up the church of Your Son Jesus. Help us to be yielded channels of Your gifts of love. Please clear out all the debris that may be clogging the sweet flow of Your Holy Spirit. Help us to have wisdom and spiritual good manners so that these gifts will be administered effectively. Thank You, Father, for all Your good gifts. In the name of Your Son, Jesus, I pray. Amen.

Scripture

"He that believeth on me, as the scripture hath said, out of his belly shall flow rivers of living water." (John 7:38)

Commentary

The leader will share from the Commentary found at the beginning of the chapter, and add to it as he or she feels led.

Prayer and Praise

Suggested songs: "Give Me Oil in My Lamp," "We'll Give the Glory to Jesus," "My Lord Is Real," "Shut In With God." Praise the Lord together, and if there is freedom, sing with the Spirit for a bit. Let the Holy Spirit refresh you physically as well as spiritually. Now break up into small discussion groups.

Small-Group Discussion

1. The gift of tongues, with interpretation, may be manifested in either one of two directions. What are these? Why is it important to recognize them both?

2. In what way may the gift of tongues be a sign to an unbeliever? Give a personal example if you have one.

3. In what way may the gift of tongues be a help to the believer? Give a personal example if you have one.

4. What are some of the mistaken ideas some have about the use of the Pentecost experience?

5. Were the languages spoken by the people on the Day of Pentecost for the purpose of proclaiming the Gospel to foreigners who were listening? Discuss.

6. You are in a meeting, and someone speaks in tongues very briefly. The interpretation, however, is very long, much longer than the speaking in tongues. How might this be explained?

7. A person comes to a meeting and says, "I have a very important decision to make, so will you please pray that there will be a message in tongues and interpretation to answer it for me?" What would your response be, if you were leading the meeting?

8. A Christian friend says, "When I need guidance, I speak in tongues and interpret, and the Lord tells me what to do." What counsel would you give him or her?

9. If you were a member of a church which did not understand or accept the gifts of the Spirit, should you be submitted to the headship of the pastor as to public manifestation of the gifts in his church?

10. If you could not submit to this pastor's leadership, what should you do? Discuss.

11. In the above situation, would the pastor or any organization have the right to ask you to refrain from private prayer in tongues? Would this be "godly admonition," and would you have to comply? Give Scripture.

12. Should you ever give up speaking in tongues for any reason?

13. How can you prepare yourself to be used in the gifts of utterance, as God so directs?

14. Have any of God's gifts been manifested through you this week? Ever?

Conclusion

Large group resumes for sharing and praise. The tape recording may be used. During the time of praise, the gifts of the Spirit should be expected and encouraged.

Practical Application

Are you using your "prayer language" regularly? If not, make it a practice to speak in tongues for at least five minutes or so every two or three hours during the day, and during your regular prayer times. See what effect this has in keeping you refreshed and aware of God's Presence through the day.

Have you ever sung "in or with" the Spirit (in tongues) ? Even people who normally can't carry a tune may easily sing in this new way. If you don't have freedom yet in speaking in tongues, it may be easier for you to begin by singing in tongues.

If you find you can't yet sing in tongues, then just sing in your own language—words of praise—letting the Holy Spirit guide the melody. After taking this one step, you may easily move over into singing in tongues. "Rejoice in the Lord."

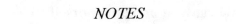
NOTES

SECTION II /SESSION 8

CHAPTER 8

THE GIFT OF PROPHECY

Moses prayed, "Would that all God's people were prophets, and that the Lord would put His Spirit upon them!" Paul said, "Desire spiritual gifts, but rather that you may prophesy." What is prophecy? Does it happen in your church? Do *you* do it? The Scripture seems to consider it very important. Some equate it with witnessing, or preaching, but a careful study of the Bible will show that while these may include prophecy, it is definitely a manifestation distinct from these and of prime importance.

Prophetic speaking at a meeting of believers brings a sense of God's immediate presence. It is mainly for "edification, exhortation, and comfort," which in the Greek means, "building up, urging on, and consoling."

God can use prophecy to foretell coming events, and to direct Christians as to how to deal with them, but where this happens, it is a confirmation of something God has been showing in other ways, and is now *underlining* by prophecy. Believers should never follow the bare words of a prophetic message. They must have a definite witness in their own spirits to its accuracy; it must fit in with other things that God is showing; and it must be in keeping with the Scripture.

To help people step out in faith to bring prophecy, be sure to let someone know if words they have spoken in the Spirit have been a help and inspiration to you. Remember also that just because a prophecy isn't meaningful for you, doesn't mean others weren't helped by it. If someone speaks in prophecy for the first time, even though in a halting manner, they should never be discussed or criticized, but commended and encouraged. The validity of a prophecy does not depend on the person bringing it. In fact, the words of a person often used in this gift should be just as carefully evaluated as those of a novice, because the assembly is likely to have more confidence in the experienced person, and feel that the words must be entirely from God. Though the gifts are pure, the human instruments used are not. Those who often prophesy should be encouraged to pray for others to be used in this gift.

Questions for Your Home Study

1. a. Did the apostle Paul consider prophecy to be an important gift? Give Scripture. _____

    b. Define the gift of prophecy. _____

2. The person who speaks in tongues (in private prayer) is speaking to _____ , but the person who prophesies is speaking to _____ , and bringing them words of _____ _____ , and

3. Speaking in tongues without interpretation should be done in private, because it builds up _____ _____ , but prophecy builds up

4. What is the difference between conditional and unconditional prophecy? Give Scriptures._____

5. Was Jesus a Prophet? Give Scripture._____

6. What is the limit to the number of prophecies in a meeting? _____

7. What is one of the primary safeguards for the gift of prophecy? _____

    _____

    _____

8. Should the words of a person who is often used in prophecy be judged less, or more than ordinary?

    _____

    _____

9. Should every believer expect to prophesy at some time in his or her life? Give Scripture, Old and New Testament. _____

    _____

10. What is good preparation for being used effectively in the gift of prophecy? _____

    _____

    _____

11. Does the Scripture expect women to prophesy? Children and youth? Give Scriptures to support your answers. _____

    _____

    _____

12. Why is it good for a woman to wait and pray for a man to participate if another woman has preceded

her? What should she do if a man is still not yielded after she has waited a reasonable time? _____

_____

13. In addition to a woman being submitted to leadership if she is going to pray or prophesy in the group, another prerequisite for the married woman is that she be submitted to _____

_____

(See Eph. 5:22; I Cor. 11:3-5.)

14. Should men also be submitted to authorized leadership, or is this instruction only valid for the women? (See Heb. 13:7,17.)_____

_____

_____

15. List as many points as you can in recognizing a false prophet. _____

_____

_____

_____

16. What is the supreme test of the validity of all spoken gifts? Why?_____

_____

Large-Group Meeting

Prayer

May we have the faith, dear Lord, to step out and let the Holy Spirit give us Your words to speak to Your people. We need to hear from You, not just now and then, but regularly. Speak to us by Your living word of prophecy. Thank You, Father, thank You, Jesus,' thank You, Holy Spirit.

Scripture

"And it shall come to pass in the last days, saith God, I will pour out of my Spirit upon all flesh: and your sons and your daughters shall prophesy . . . And on my servants and on my handmaidens I will pour out in those days of my spirit; and they shall prophesy." (Acts 2:17-18)

Commentary

The leader will share from the Commentary found at the beginning of the chapter and add to it as he or she feels led.

Prayer and Praise

Suggested songs: "Trust in the Lord With All Thy Heart," "Rivers Shall Flow in the Wilderness," "Oh Glory, Glory, Glory!," "Fresh Oil from the Throne." After prayer and praise, break up into small discussion groups.

Small-Group Discussion

1. Can prophecy be corrective? Will it be condemnatory or harsh? Why, or why not?

2. What is the basic difference between those who prophesied in the Old Testament and those who prophesied in the New Testament?

3. Differentiate between prophecy, teaching, and preaching. How are they related?

4. How should "directive prophecy" be safeguarded? Why should it be received with caution?

5. What is one of the main purposes of the "unconditional" prophecies of the Bible?

6. Some say that *witnessing* is prophecy. Do you agree? Why, or why not?

7. Because there has been some misuse of the gift of prophecy in the past, should Christians today reject this gift of utterance? What can we do to keep the past mistakes from recurring?

8. Does a Christian who is walking in the Spirit need to be concerned that he might bring counterfeit prophecy? Through whom do counterfeits come?

9. Has prophecy in a meeting ever been a help to you or to someone else you know of?

10. Have you noticed any difference in your life since you've been praying and / or singing in your Holy Spirit language daily? What has happened?

Conclusion

Large group resumes for sharing and praise. The tape may be played. During praise time, expect the Holy Spirit to manifest the gift you have been studying about!

Practical Application

Have you ever ministered gifts of utterance? Which ones? If not, have you ever asked God to let you do so? Why don't you?

If you have often brought gifts of utterance, for several weeks try the experiment of asking God to manifest His gifts through others in your prayer group or charismatic church. If you feel an urge to speak in tongues, interpret, or prophesy, before you speak, wait and ask God to use someone else. Pray that God's glory will be manifest in all the members of His Body.

NOTES

SECTION II /SESSION 9

CHAPTER 9

GIFTS OF HEALING

The gift of healing is the most widespread of the gifts in the New Testament. Someone estimated that Jesus spent 90 percent of His time healing the sick. The New Testament makes it abundantly clear that He healed all who asked Him, and all who were brought to Him by others. We have indication, too, that Jesus sought out the sick and healed them, as with the man at the pool of Bethesda. The Gospel of Matthew tells us that Jesus went about *all* the cities and villages, teaching in their synagogues, and preaching the Gospel of the kingdom, and healing *every* sickness and *every* disease among the people. We need never have any hesitation about whether God wants to heal the sick, for the Scripture makes it completely clear that He always wants to. When there is an apparent failure of healing prayer, it is never because God does not want to heal, but because there is a block somewhere that is keeping the person from receiving the healing that God wants to give. It is no wonder that someone who has never heard that Jesus still heals today, or worse yet, who has continually been taught the opposite, should have difficulty believing for healing in time of need. Therefore, our best efforts in ministering God's healing should be directed at increasing the faith of the person we are ministering to—faith that God is ready and willing to heal him or her.

Jesus healed the sick because, first of all, He had compassion on them. Our desire to heal should arise, first of all, from our compassion for those who are suffering. The greatest purpose of healing the sick is to let people see Jesus at work, in order that the unbeliever may accept Him, and in order that the believer may have his or her faith strengthened in the joy of God's love. Obviously we must not look at healing as an end in itself—we do not receive Jesus in order to have a kind of insurance policy against sickness. That would be a shaky foundation for faith! Our faith does not *depend* on healing. If it does, we are likely to be angry with God if sickness comes, instead of trusting God, and receiving healing for ourselves or helping others to receive their healing.

Certainly the most wonderful thing of all is to discover Jesus as the Healer of our spirits and souls, bringing us "joy unspeakable and full of glory," but how wonderful it is that our Lord wants to bring life and joy to our physical bodies, too! We are three-part creatures, and our Lord wants to bless our whole being—spirit, soul, and body.

Questions for Your Home Study

1. What is one of the most widely accepted gifts of
    the Holy Spirit today? Why do you suppose this
    is? _____

    _____

2. How long has Jesus' ministry of healing been going
    on? When will it cease? _____

    _____

3. Do you think that a person who is used to bringing
    gifts of healing should claim permanently to have
    the ability to heal, or to be a "healer"? Why, or
    why not? _____

    _____

4. A person can be healed through _____
    when he is too ill and weak to exercise his own
    faith. He can be healed through _____
    alone. Most desirably, healing comes through the
    combined faith of the _____
    and the _____

    _____

5. Before praying for a sick person to be healed, what
    are some faith-building Scriptures you might share
    with him? _____

    _____

    _____

6. Can you find a Scripture anywhere in the Bible that says God wants His *faithful* people to be sick and in pain? _____

_____

_____

7. Did Jesus ever refuse to heal anyone who came to Him or was brought to Him? Who were the only ones He could not heal? Why? (See Mark 6.)

_____

_____

8. What are some of the other gifts in addition to healing itself that may be needed when praying for the sick? _____

_____

_____

9. Often there is a "chain reaction," and a person may be healed at the same time he is _____ or _____

10. What should be the most important result of healing in the life of an unbeliever? _____

_____

Large-Group Meeting

Prayer

Dear Father, as believer priests we have received the very garment of Jesus' life! As we walk through this sick world, may the hem of our garments touch many lives to bring them wholeness. A handful of people alone cannot do the job You're counting on us to do; may multitudes of Your people become healing channels of God's great love. In Jesus' name. Amen.

Scripture

"A woman, which was diseased . . . twelve years, came behind him, and touched the hem of his garment: For she said within herself, if I may but touch his garment, I shall be whole. But Jesus turned . . . about, and when he saw her, he said, `Daughter, be of good comfort; thy faith hath made thee whole.'" (Matt. 9:20-22) "Put ye on the Lord Jesus Christ . . ." (Rom. 13:14a)

Commentary

The leader will share from the Commentary found at the beginning of the chapter, and add to it as he or she feels led.

Prayer and Praise

Suggested songs: "Oh, It Is Jesus," "There's a River of Life," "Spring Up, O Well." After a time of prayer and praise, break up into small discussion groups.

Small-Group Discussion

1. Discuss John 14:12. Does this apply to us today? Would it include healing?

2. How can you begin to be used in the gifts of healing? What is a good way to prepare yourself?

3. What are some of the various ways in which Jesus healed the sick—that is, what outward actions did He take? What should this teach us today?

4. What are some of the obstacles to a present-day believer accepting healing for himself? How can these obstacles be removed?

5. If you counsel with a person, and he or she confesses his sins to God in your presence, and you are able to assure him of God's forgiveness, should you then
a) Share this confession with your pastor, getting his advice about how to help the person further;
b) Talk it over with your wife or husband, or someone else whose judgment you value;
c) Keep it completely confidential, asking God to help you forget it entirely.

6. Do you think the healing of the soul (psychological nature: intellect, will, emotions) is important, as well as healing of the body? Is it sometimes overlooked?

7. What do you think of a person who prays for the sick, but has not received Jesus as Savior, and does not believe He is God's only begotten Son come in the flesh? Should you let such a person pray for

you, or encourage anyone else to go to him or her? Why or why not?

8. Have you seen any results after you prayed for the gifts of utterance to be manifested in your life or others? (Be sure to keep an attitude of expectation in these areas.)

Conclusion

Large group resumes for sharing and praise. The tape may be played. After singing and rejoicing, the leader may ask for those who need prayer for healing and believe that they are ready to *receive* to lift their right hand. While their hands are lifted, he (or someone else he designates) should pray a prayer of faith for the group. Following this, he might want to ask for testimonies on the spot as to those who have been touched by Jesus. Faith should have been built during the session and many made ready to receive healing.

Practical Application

Make it your practice to pray for healing needs at home, even very small things—a bumped head or a scratched knee. Expect to see God's glory. Be sensitive to the Holy Spirit's leading to pray for the sick, anywhere, anytime.

Several of you may want to begin a library of faithbuilding healing testimonies and teachings on tape cassettes to lend to people who are ill. Cassette tape recorders for "playback only" are quite reasonable.

Some may be led to develop a hospital ministry this way. If your minister believes in healing, he may appreciate your assistance in calling on the sick.

NOTES

SECTION II / SESSION 10

CHAPTER IO

THE WORKING OF MIRACLES

The Bible is full of miracles. A miracle is a sign of God's sovereign power-it is God changing His usual pattern of doing things in accord with the request of His son or daughter. A miracle is not done primarily to impress people, but to meet a need. When believers, and those ready to believe, see a miracle, it brings faith, or strengthens it. When a willful unbeliever sees a miracle, he ignores it or explains it away. Miracles don't prove holiness or merit on the part of the person involved, but do prove faith.

Each believer should be expecting a miracle, not only every day, but many times a day. Many miracles are small ones, and we should be alert not to miss them, glorify God for them, and let them build our faith. God absolutely loves to perform miracles for and through His children. If our faith remains as a little child's, we will live in a world of wonder.

Questions for Your Home Study

1. What is a miracle? _____

    _____

2. What would be a better way to describe what we call the "laws of nature"? _____

    _____

    _____

3. What is the analogy between the relationship of Elijah and Elisha, and between Jesus Christ and the believer today? What Scripture would you quote to illustrate this? _____

    _____

    _____

4. Distinguish between the gift of miracles and the gifts of healing. _____

    _____

    _____

5. Who performed the most miracles in the Bible? Name others in the Scripture who performed miracles? _____

    _____

6. Give three examples of miracles Jesus performed. (Give more if you wish.) _____

   _____

   _____

7. a. Give several biblical examples of miracles performed through believers after Pentecost.

   _____

   _____

   _____

   b. Give an example you have read about or know of personally, where a believer in the twentieth century has experienced a miracle (or miracles).

   _____

   _____

   _____

8. Is the raising of the dead a miracle or a healing? Or? _____

   _____

9. Are the "greater things" Jesus talks about in John *more striking* things, or just *more* things?_____

   _____

10. Is there any reason to believe that manifestations of God's power are supposed to die away in the believer's life as he or she becomes more "mature"? Give Scripture from the Book of Acts to support your answer. _____

   _____

   _____

Large-Group Meeting

Prayer

You are a God of miracles, Father, and everything You do is wonderful. May we expect You to work miracles in and through us, so that we may begin to experience that dominion and victory over circumstances that You gave us in our creation, and re-established in a far higher way when You took us to be Your children through Jesus Christ. Amen.

Scripture

"Verily I say unto you, Except ye be converted, and become as little children, ye shall not enter into the kingdom of heaven." (Matt. 18.3) "Call unto me, and I will answer thee, and shew thee great and mighty things, which thou knowest not." (Jer. 33:3)

Commentary

The leader will share from the Commentary found at the beginning of the chapter, and add to it as he or she feels led.

Prayer and Praise

Suggested songs: "Call Unto Me," "Blessed Be the Lord God of Israel," "Miracles Can Happen." When you learn "Miracles Can Happen" by heart, put down your books and do something else new and yet old—

clap your hands! Psalm 47:1 says "Clap your hands, *all* ye people." This is childlike and frees inhibited people. Give it a try! After a period of prayer and praise, break into small discussion groups.

Small-Group Discussion

1. List six miracles in the Old Testament. Although God is all-powerful, do you see in each of these cases He is counting on one of His people to work together with Him?

2. Why do people experience many miracles right after the Baptism in the Holy Spirit, and then tend to see fewer of them? Is this normal? How can it be avoided?

3. What were Jesus' motives for doing His miracles?

4. If someone says, "We are not supposed to expect signs! It says in the Bible that it's wrong to believe God will give signs today!" How do you answer these objections? Give Scripture.

5. Where have striking manifestations of miracles been taking place in the world today? Why? What might help more of such things to happen in our own country, as well as in other places?

6. Does a miracle prove the work, the validity of the teachings, or the worthiness of the person performing it? What test is to be applied? Give Scripture.

7. What dangers are there in God's people experiencing the miraculous? Should these dangers cause us not to desire miracles? What precautions can be taken against these problems?

8. Can Satan counterfeit God's miracles? Give examples. How can we tell the difference between God's true work and Satan's counterfeit?

9. Have you personally witnessed a miracle? Tell about it.

10. Were you or anyone you know of, healed at last week's   class or following it? Did you have the opportunity to pray personally for someone this week to be healed? If so, how did you go about it? Have you made any plans to help bring the message of Jesus' healing power to those in need?

Conclusion

The whole group comes back together to share the fresh insights of the small groups. The cassette tape may be played. The meeting concludes with a further time of praise and prayer. You have been talking about miracles—faith has been built. Expect God to do miracles right here and now!

Practical Application

Be watching for little miracles in your life this week. Watch for the "coincidences" which are really "God's incidences"! Expect big miracles, too! The little ones build faith for the big ones. Keep a childlike attitude of expectancy.

Did you see more of the miraculous in your own life right after the Baptism in the Holy Spirit than you are seeing today? What were you doing then, that you are not doing now? What are some things in your life which may be blocking what God wants to do? What practical steps can be taken to help you cooperate more with God?

NOTES

SECTION II /SESSION 11

CHAPTER 11

THE GIFT OF FAITH

We fail to understand the meaning of many words like "love," "trust," "hope," because we tend to think of them as describing substances or essences, or perhaps states of mind, instead of seeing them as primarily things that are happening—actions. "Faith" is one of those words. "Show me your faith by your actions," says James the Apostle. To "have faith" is to be actively trusting. Faith undergirds all other manifestations of the Spirit. None of the others will function without it, and we must exercise it in order to receive the others.

After, by our faith, we have received Jesus; the *fruit* of faith begins to grow and increase in our lives. The *gift* of faith is different from the slowly growing fruit, in that it is given instantenously when needed. It is a sudden surge of faith, usually in a crisis, to confidently believe without a doubt, that as we act or speak in Jesus' Name, and according to His Word, it will come to pass. The person experiencing this is usually surprised to realize that he had courage to step out so boldly. The gift of faith itself, of course, builds faith, and brings glory to God.

Questions for Your Home Study

1. Where is the definition of faith given in the Scriptures? Write the verse and the reference.

   _____

   _____

2. We learn three things about faith from this reference:
   a. Faith is _____ or it's not faith at all.
   b. Faith is _____ before _____
   c. Faith is _____ and not _____

3. What are the three kinds of supernatural faith?

   _____

   _____

4. How does a person obtain saving faith? _____

   _____

   _____

5. The fruit of faith comes first as a result of: reading the Bible, much prayer, being baptized in the Holy

Spirit, receiving Jesus Christ as Savior, attending church every Sunday. (Underline the correct answer.)

6. What key word describes what is necessary in order to continue to bear good fruit? (See John 15:4-8.)

_____

7. Will a person who is abiding in Christ and then is baptized in the Holy Spirit be likely to bear even more fruit? Why? _____

_____

_____

8. Define the gift of faith. _____

_____

9. The gift of faith may be manifested by being ____
   _____ as in Mark 4:35-41 or it may be_____
   _____out, as in Acts 12:11, or a
   combination of _____
   _____ and _____
   as in Acts 9:40.

10. Can you find some other examples in the Bible of things that happened through the gift of faith, in addition to those we have already mentioned in this chapter? (Use your concordance.) _____

_____

_____

11. The three gifts of power are: _____
_____ , and _____

Large-Group Meeting

Prayer

Heavenly Father, although Jesus, Your Son, was the only one to live at a full and consistent level of faith in You, yet You've set high goals for us—to keep us always looking forward and moving upward. Help us not to limit what You desire to do in and through our lives. We can do this only as we keep our eyes on Jesus and off other people and circumstances. Praise Your Name! Thank You, for helping us, Lord Jesus! Amen.

Scripture

"Brethren, I count not myself to have apprehended: but this one thing I do, forgetting those things which are behind, and reaching forth unto those things which are before, I press toward the mark for the prize of the high calling of God in Christ Jesus." (Phil. 3:13-14)

Commentary

The leader will share from the Commentary found at the beginning of the chapter, and will add to it as he or she feels led.

Prayer and Praise

Suggested songs: "Yesterday, Today, Forever," "All Things Are Possible When We Believe," "There's Never Been a Day Like This Day." After a time of praise and singing "in the Spirit," break into smaller groups for discussion.

Small-Group Discussion

1. What is natural human faith? Would you agree that it is not really faith at all?

2. Can anyone without real faith or trust in Jesus be pleasing to God? Give Scripture and discuss.

3. Have you seen and experienced the three kinds of supernatural faith in your own life? Discuss.

4. What is the basic difference between faith as a fruit and faith as a gift of the spirit?

5. Do those who have manifested strongly the gift of faith necessarily live at that level 100 percent of the time? Give several examples to support your answer from both the Old and New Testaments.

6. Distinguish between the gift of faith and the gift of miracles, and also discuss how they are interrelated.

7. From your reading, select modern examples of the spoken and acted gift of faith, or give examples from personal experience.

8. Why should the sharing of the wonderful things God has done or is doing in our lives *not* cause us to become puffed up or proud?

9. a. Have you seen or heard of any big or little miracles which occurred at the last meeting or during this week—to you or another person?

   b. If the second part of the practical application question pertained to you last week, did you make a list of the things that may be blocking the miraculous works of God in your life? Are you praying about them and taking other practical steps to be more open to God; If it wouldn't embarrass you, share your answer.

Conclusion

The large group resumes for sharing and praise. The tape may be played.

Practical Application

What can you do to help faith and trust in Jesus grow and develop in your own life? In the life of your family?

Thank and praise God for the fruit of faith that is growing in your life—whether you can see it or not! Look for opportunities to exercise your faith this week. Speak words of faith to someone who needs to hear them this week. Be expecting the gift of faith to be manifested as it's needed.

NOTES

CHAPTER 12

DISCERNING OF SPIRITS

In this permissive age, a gift such as the gift of discernment is likely to be played down. In spiritual matters, as in the world at large, moderns are inclined to feel that each has the right to "do his own thing" without interference from others. As we have seen, only too clearly, this leaves the field very clear for Satan to do *his* thing—namely, to deceive and confuse God's people. The Scripture tells us that the deceptions of the enemy are going to become more and more subtle, until he "will deceive, if it were possible, even the very elect." How important is it then to pray for and believe for the gift of discernment. Christians are needed who will be quick to respond to God, and also quick to know when things are not as they should be!

People who have been involved with the occult, or have been in drugs, alcoholism, or other deep problems, often have a greater battle extricating themselves from the inroads the enemy has made into their minds, emotions, and bodies. Even after they accept Jesus Christ, renounce all wrong activities, and receive the Baptism in the Spirit, there may still be a battle for them to regain the territory that was lost. They may look around and wonder why other Christians are not having the same battles, and even wonder if there is something lacking in their experience in Christ. If the reason for their problems is realized, this will be a tremendous help. Prayer assistance by another may be needed for some time. Total recovery is assured as they press in close to Jesus.

People who have this kind of background may understand more fully others in similar situations and be able to minister effectively to them. As the Scripture says, "Freely you have received, freely give."

Questions for Your Home Study

1. What do we mean by a "revelation gift"? Name the gifts of revelation. _____
   _____
   _____

2. From what directions can the human mind receive information besides the physical senses? Which is lawful and which unlawful? _____
   _____
   _____

3. What is natural discernment? Why is it unreliable?
   _____
   _____

4. Is true intellectual discernment important? How can we grow in it? _____
   _____
   _____

5. Why is the gift of discerning of spirits so important to the Christian fellowship? Give two opposite reasons. _____
   _____
   _____

6. What did Wigglesworth mean when he said that the gift of the discerning of spirits is not the gift of criticism? _____
   _____
   _____

7. Give three examples of the discerning of evil spirits from Scripture. _____
   _____
   _____

The Holy Spirit and You

8. Can a Christian be possessed by a wrong spirit?
_____
_____

9. How could wrong spirits affect a Christian? How
would they get a chance to do so? _____
_____
_____

10. How does a Christian prepare himself or herself
before praying with someone for deliverance?
_____
_____

11. What are some important steps to remember when
praying with another for deliverance? Write as
many as you can. _____
_____
_____
_____
_____

12. Must there be a physical manifestation (coughing,
sobbing, retching, etc.) when a wrong spirit is cast
out? Do such manifestations sometimes take place?
_____
_____

13. Is it important to have the cooperation of the person
when praying for deliverance for them? _____
_____
_____

14. What must we be sure to ask for after deliverance is accomplished? Why is this prayer important?

_____

_____

15. Is it a good idea to "specialize" in a deliverance ministry? Why or why not?_____

_____

_____

16. Should every Christian be prepared to pray for deliverance? _____

_____

_____

Large-Group Meeting

Prayer

Dear God, Thank You for not leaving Your children helpless in the darkness of this world. Thank You for providing us with the gift of discernment to protect us, especially in this day and hour. Help more of Your children to be aware of and to believe for this important gift, so that we can bring light into darkness, dispelling the works of the enemy. In Jesus' name. Amen.

Scripture

Jesus said, "As long as I am in the world, I am the light of the world." (John 9:5)

Jesus said to His people, "Ye are the light of the world. A city that is set on a hill cannot be hid . . . Let your light so shine before men, that they may see your good works, and glorify your Father which is in heaven." (Matt. 5:14, 16)

Commentary

The leader will share from the Commentary found at the beginning of the chapter, and will add to it as he or she feels led.

Prayer and Praise

Suggested songs: "It Is the Time to Take the Kingdom," "Greater Is He That Is Within You," "Jesus Breaks Every Fetter." After a time of prayer and praise, break into small groups for discussion.

Small-Group Discussion

1. Give an example of Satan's counterfeit of discernment other than the example given in *The Holy Spirit and You.*

2. If you discerned that there was something wrong in a meeting, what could you do about it without violating "decency and order"?

3. Have you ever manifested the gift of discerning evil spirits? How did your own spirit feel? What were you able to do about it?

4. You are praying with someone for deliverance from an obsession. You have discerned that it is a spirit of fear that is tormenting him or her. The person prays, "Oh God, please help this spirit of fear to be cast away from me. Dear Jesus I pray this under the power of Your Blood!" Would you accept this as an effective deliverance prayer, or would you ask them to say it differently? How? Explain why, or why not. (See page 156)

5. Some teach that faithful believers are being continuously beset by evil spirits, and must constantly be casting them out of themselves and others. Comment on this. Is it a half-truth? Is it not true at all?

6. If a person keeps returning for deliverance prayer time and time again with little or no improvement, what could be lacking? (Also see John 8:31-32.)

7. Did you see any new growth in your faith and trust in Jesus in this past week? Were you able to help build the faith of another, or were you used in the gift of faith ?

Conclusion

The large group resumes for sharing and praise. The tape may be used.

Since deliverance prayer should normally be done in private, the leader may ask for those who feel the need for individual help to remain after dismissal. The large-group leader should be competent in this area or should in advance of the meeting ask some reputable person who is, to stay to lead this time of prayer. Others who have been used effectively in this ministry may be asked to stay to assist the leader also. For those who can't stay longer but need help, private appointments should be made quickly—before this prayer time.

Practical Application

In your private prayer, seek to increase your sensitivity to God, and your response to Him in the Holy Spirit. Pay attention to the Holy Spirit's discernment of wrong things. Do not ignore feelings of uneasiness about situations, but pay attention to them, and ask the Lord to show you what they mean.

Are you willing to be an instrument to set captives free? Tell the Lord that you are willing, and know that He will provide the situation when you are ready. Then just keep your eyes on Jesus.

Married couples who are both baptized in the Spirit thus freer in their prayer life with one another—will find they have a wonderful combination for prayer help. When hurtful memories of the past or wrong habit patterns crop up in one's life, it is usually known by the other partner; this is an excellent time to pray for one another in the privacy of your own home. After such prayer, lay hands on one another to pray for a renewed filling of the Holy Spirit, then praise God together in the Spirit. Others who do not have this kind of situation, can pray in the same way with a close friend (preferably of the same sex) who has proved trustworthy.

NOTES

CHAPTER 13

THE "WORD OF KNOWLEDGE" AND THE "WORD OF WISDOM"

We now come to the end of the chapters on the gifts of the Holy Spirit with a study of the gifts of the "word of wisdom" and the "word of knowledge." These gifts are fragments of God's wisdom and knowledge shared with the believer to meet specific needs and situations. These manifestations do not necessarily have to be spoken, or even be in verbal form—the Greek "*logos*," which is here translated "word," means "matter," or "concern," so wisdom and knowledge can be given in many forms. God gives just what is needed, because He knows that we cannot be trusted with more! Our spirits have been reborn in the Holy Spirit, but our souls and bodies are still in the process of being put back in order, and we cannot be trusted with such powers and abilities under our own control.

The so-called psychics are those who are trying to gain their own control over supernatural wisdom and knowledge, and they open themselves to Satan, who is eager to give human beings the illusion that they can manipulate these powers, to feed their pride, and to delude them, and the world through them. It is, after all, the same theme that Satan used to draw our first ancestors away from God, and our enemy well knows how human beings can be attracted by such things. Let us beware of falling into his trap, and let us warn others also. Let us turn toward God, and accept the good and wholesome gifts He has for us.

Christian believers should expect to manifest the gifts of wisdom and knowledge, just as they expect the other gifts. They should apply to them the same kind of tests and precautions as they do to the other gifts: Is it scriptural? Does my spirit witness to it? Is it loving? Helpful? Does it create order rather than confusion, harmony rather than discord, etc.?

Questions for Your Home Study

1. Define the "word of knowledge." What are three purposes for which this gift is used? _____

   _____

   _____

2. Define the "word of wisdom." _____

   _____

   _____

3. Which of these two gifts is the most important?

   _____

4. Must the gifts of the "word of knowledge" and the "word of wisdom" necessarily be spoken, in order for them to be manifested? Explain. _____

   _____

   _____

5. What does the absence of the article in the Greek describing the gifts of knowledge and wisdom serve to remind us? _____

   _____

   _____

   _____

6. If you receive a "word of knowledge," in order to know how to apply it, what should you do? _____

   _____

   _____

7. List a number of ways in which these gifts may be made known to you. _____

   _____

   _____

8. Natural human knowledge often creates great ____

   _____

   so that some people are kept from entering into __
   the _____

   _____

9. Compare man's wisdom to God's wisdom. _____

_____

_____

_____

10. What were the counterfeit gifts Satan used to tempt the first man and woman? Name some practices which fall into these categories. _____

_____

_____

_____

11. The gifts of the "word of knowledge" and "the word of wisdom "do not involve human _____

12. Write the Scripture that tells you that God is ready to give you all the wisdom you need. _____

_____

_____

13. Give some scriptural examples of the "word of knowledge." _____

_____

_____

_____

14. Give some scriptural examples of the "word of wisdom." _____

_____

_____

15. The three categories we are using for the nine gifts
of the Holy Spirit are:
Gifts of _____
Gifts of _____
Gifts of _____

16. Since it is true that all of the supernatural
happenings in the Bible (excluding counterfeits,
naturally) can be identified with one or another of
the nine gifts of the Holy Spirit listed in I Cor.
12:7-11, would you say that this is the most
definitive listing of the gifts in the Scriptures?

_____

_____

17. Is it probable that all nine gifts would be manifested
through a Christian in one meeting? Why, or why
not?_____

_____

18. Is it scriptural to believe that all nine gifts could
be manifested through a Christian during a period
of several years? Why, or why not?_____

_____

19. Why does God desire the gifts to be active in His
children's lives?_____

_____

Large-Group Meeting

Prayer

Dear Father God, You are King of the universe and want Your children to ask largely of You for the gifts provided for us to live victorious Christian lives! Forgive us for often living as spiritual paupers, when You have provided such a super-abundance! You truly are our *Father*. Thank You so much; we love and praise You. In Jesus' name. Amen.

Scripture

"But as it is written, Eye hath not seen, nor ear heard, neither have entered into the heart of man, the things which God hath prepared for them that love him." (I Cor. 2:9)

"For ye see your calling, brethren, how that not many wise men after the flesh, not many mighty, not many noble, are called: But God hath chosen the foolish things of the world to confound the wise; and God hath chosen the weak things of the world to confound the things which are mighty; And base things of the world, and things which are despised, hath God chosen, yea, and things which are not, to bring to nought things that are: That no flesh should glory in his presence." (I Cor. 1:26-29)

Commentary

The leader will share from the Commentary found at the beginning of the chapter, and will add to it as he or she feels led.

Summary

Although we have encouraged baptized-in-the-Spirit believers to be open for all of the gifts of the Spirit over a period of time, yet we need to say also that not every one *has* to manifest all these gifts. Not every Christian will even *want* to express all the gifts, and no one should be made to feel obligated to feel that they have to do so. It looks as though Saint Paul himself didn't manifest the gift of tongues in the public assembly, choosing rather to prophesy, speak by revelation through other gifts, or to teach; he did, however, pray in tongues in private more than any in the Corinthian church (I Cor. 14:18-19).

On the other hand, for those who *want to* believe God for all the gifts of the Holy Spirit—and many have—they should be encouraged and not discouraged from doing so. "According to their faith be it unto them!" Saint Paul himself said only to follow him as he followed Christ, and we need to remember that we, too, are also to follow Christ and *His* leading for our individual lives. Often the gifts of the Spirit will occur in different patterns, but generally speaking, after experiencing the gifts of utterance, you should look forward to the gifts of power and of revelation to be added—not leaving the first ones behind, of course, but entering into more of what God has for you. The Holy Spirit wants us to be flexible, able to function in many ways—thus being much more effective for God than we ever dreamed possible.

Let us believe largely for what God has for us, being careful not to compare ourselves with others, thus limiting what God may want to do in our individual lives. Let us stretch ourselves to believe for and prepare for those greater things Jesus promised we would do before His return!

Prayer and Praise

Suggested songs: "Exceedingly Abundantly," "Confidence" no. 114, "It's All in Thee" no. 104. After prayer and praise, break into small discussion groups.

Small-Group Discussion

1. Discuss the difference between what we have called "true intellectual knowledge," and the "word of knowledge."

2. Do you think Paul was speaking of wisdom and knowledge, the spiritual gifts, when he said that we have "the mind of Christ"? Why, or why not?

3. Have you ever been put "on the spot" for your faith and had the gifts of knowledge and wisdom given to you at that moment? Tell about it. Or give examples of other times when these gifts were manifested in your life.

4. Do you know someone personally who has manifested false supernatural knowledge? Tell about it. What did you do or could you do to extricate them from such deceptions?

5. How do you think the "word of knowledge" and the "word of wisdom" relate to the gift of prophecy?

6. Why doesn't God give His people the ability to foretell the future, to read minds, to have access to supernatural knowledge in general? Why does He mete it out in small portions?

7. What would you say to someone who says, "I want God to give me the gift of knowledge!" or "I have three of the gifts, now I want to get some more."

8. How do you test the validity of these gifts of wisdom and knowledge? How would the tests compare with the judging of prophecy?

9. Have you had the experience of discerning a wrong spirit in a person's life, and praying for deliverance for that person? Share it with the group—omitting names and places, of course.

Conclusion

The large group resumes for sharing and praise. The tape may be played. During praise time, some people, because of their increased faith, may see or know something in the Spirit they wouldn't share unless the leader encouraged them. He may ask those so moved to speak out what they feel the Lord is or has been showing them that evening (if they feel it is for the group). Others there may have further understanding of what has been shown and can share that also. People who receive wisdom or knowledge during a meeting may find it more helpful to write it down and hand it to the leader for him to evaluate before sharing with the group. As you can see, these gifts of knowledge and wisdom are a bit more difficult to share, and that's one of the reasons they have not been heard from so often in the past. With sensitive leadership, these gifts can be encouraged.

Practical Application

Read through the Gospels of Mark and Luke, indicating in your Bible when you find one of the gifts of revelation. Do the same with the other Gospels and also other parts of the Bible as you find time to do so. Look also for the other gifts of the Holy Spirit as you do your daily Scripture reading.

If you haven't already done so, tell the Lord that you are willing to let these gifts of knowledge and wisdom manifest in your life to His glory. The best way to begin to let this happen is to attend a small charismatic prayer meeting. There it will be easier to share what God is trying to show you. If there isn't one in your area, you and a few other families might want to start one. All who expect to manifest the gifts should have taken some time to study what God's Word has to say about them. (The last two chapters of the textbook will give you some pointers on home prayer meetings.)

NOTES

SECTION III / SESSION 14

CHAPTER 14

THE EXCELLENT WAY

The Old Testament priest had a ministry in two directions: to God, and to the people of God. Each Christian believer today is also a priest to God, and to the people. The high priest in earlier days wore a garment called the robe of the ephod, and around the hem of it were golden bells and pomegranates. (The pomegranates were probably represented by embroidery, or perhaps of metal, but the bells were real bells.) We may see these as prophetic of the gifts and fruit of the Spirit that were to be manifested by the new priesthood of Christ in His people. The bells announced the entrance of the properly vested high priest into the Holy Place to minister to God, but they also signaled to the people outside the tabernacle that their high priest was ministering and interceding for them, although they could not see him. In these days of the new priesthood in Jesus, the gifts announce to God that we are properly vested—that is, that we are trusting His Son, and that His compassion and power are being shown through us in the gifts of the Spirit. The manifestation of the gifts show to the people "outside" that Jesus is alive, and that He is in us.

"Blessed are the people that hear the joyful sound." The ringing of bells is usually associated with joy. "God is gone up with a merry noise!" says the Psalmist (Ps. 47:5 Coverdale Version in *The Book of Common Prayer),* speaking prophetically of the Ascension of Jesus; and on the Day of Pentecost, when the Holy Spirit was poured out upon all flesh, there was a "merry noise," as the disciples began to praise and glorify God. The lookers-on saw clearly that Jesus was alive in the disciples, and they wanted to share in the rejoicing, too.. Jesus has been waiting ever since then to return to this earth. One of the signs of His soon return is that the gifts of the Spirit are once more being manifested in an increasing intensity. As men and women are responding to the Holy Spirit in their hearts, the golden bells are once more ringing out, announcing that Jesus is alive, and that the way is being prepared for His return. The nearer that day comes, the more clear and beautiful will be the ringing of the bells!

As great as this picture is, the world won't see Jesus alive and in us without the fruit of the Spirit. Only with the pomegranates between the bells will the bells ring in harmony and beauty as they were intended to. It isn't a matter of needing the fruit *or* the gifts—*-both* *are* imperative if we are going to live the most effective possible Christian lives. The excellent way must include both the fruit and the gifts functioning together in each believer in as unadulterated a manner as possible!

Questions for Your Home Study

1. Why are bells a fitting symbol of the gifts of the Spirit? _____
    _____

2. Why are pomegranates a fitting symbol of the fruit of the Holy Spirit? _____
    _____

3. Read I Cor. 13, and make a list of the things this chapter tells us about love—what it is, and what it does. _____
    _____
    _____

4. Draw a large oval and list the gifts and fruit of the Holy Spirit around it alternately, symbolizing the robe of the ephod.

5. In what way does this pattern of the alternate bells and pomegranates carry over into the New Testament? _____

_____

_____

6. What symbolic inference may be drawn from the fact that the Scripture speaks of the "fruit" of the Spirit, instead of the "fruits" of the Spirit?

_____

_____

7. What are the two words for "love" used in the New Testament? Discuss their meanings.

_____

_____

_____

8. Which kind of love is I Corinthians 13 speaking of? _____

_____

9. What is the new commandment that Jesus has given us, His people?_____

_____

10. How long will the gifts of the Spirit be needed? When will they pass away? _____

_____

_____

11. What does the ringing of the golden bells proclaim to the world about our Great High Priest today?

_____

_____

12. Is it possible to manifest gifts of the Spirit without bearing fruit? Give Scripture. Would anyone want to do this? _____

_____

_____

13. Is it true that love is the greatest gift of the Spirit? Why, or why not? _____

_____

_____

14. How many gifts of the Spirit did you find in the Gospel of Saint Mark? What were some of them?

_____

_____

_____

Large-Group Meeting

Prayer

Dear God, thank You that when You gave us Your only begotten Son, You gave us *agape*—love of the highest kind —the kind of love that loves because it is its nature to love, and not for any other reason. Thank You that Jesus could love the unlovely and the unworthy, because He is love, and therefore that He came to save us, while we were yet sinners. Thank You that this kind of love dwells in us through Jesus, by the power of the Spirit. May we not try to keep this love to ourselves, but share it with all with whom we come in contact, by letting Jesus love them through us. Make us channels of Your love through which all the other fruit and gifts may flow. Praise to You, Lord! In Jesus' wonderful name.

Scripture

"Love is patient and kind; love is not envious; love is not puffed up with pride, does not behave itself unmannerly or out of order, seeks not her own way, is not easily irritated, entertains no evil thoughts . . . rejoices when right and truth win; love is consistent, love is always ready to trust, expects the best in everything, endures as a good soldier. Love never ends." (I Cor. 13:4-8a Author's paraphrase, quoted from *The Holy Spirit and You*, p. 179-180)

Commentary

The leader will share from the Commentary found at the beginning of the chapter, and add to it as he or she feels led.

Prayer and Praise

Suggested songs: "His Banner Over Me Is Love," "This Is My Commandment," "The Peace of God." After prayer and praise, break into small discussion groups.

Small-Group Discussion

1. Compare the purpose of the golden bells around the robe of the high priest with the function of the gifts in the believer's life today. What does the functioning of the gifts tell us about Jesus?

2. How would you answer this statement: "The thirteenth chapter of I Corinthians teaches that the gifts—specifically, prophecy, tongues, and knowledge—have all passed away because we now have 'that which is perfect' which replaces them— namely, the Bible."

3. What are the dangers of having gifts without the fruit?

4. What are the dangers of having fruit without gifts?

5. How do you answer someone who says, "You take the gifts, I'll take the fruit"?

6. How effective do you think Jesus' own ministry would have been if He had manifested only the fruit of the Spirit and none of the gifts?

7. Describe the difference between those who have ministered the gifts as golden bells and those who have sounded like clanging brass bells. How can the latter be helped?

8. How would you counsel a Christian who claims he hates himself? What does self-hate keep a Christian from doing?

Conclusion

The large group resumes for sharing, tape, and praise. During the praise time, the leader may ask everyone to close their eyes so no one will be embarrassed, and then ask those who have difficulty feeling loved and who want to be healed to raise a hand to signify their need. Asking all the people across the rows to join hands, he may pray a prayer of faith for the healing of the emotions of these people. Some may want to stay later for further prayer help.

Practical Application

Read through the Gospels of Mark and Luke again and mark everywhere you find the fruit of the Spirit being expressed. You may want to do the same thing with the other Gospels.

If you have had difficulty believing that God loves you, then look up Scriptures which tell that He loves you, and write the verses out for easy reference, keeping them in a handy spot. For several weeks or longer read these verses over—out loud, if possible.

When is the last time you verbalized your love to your mate, children, other close family members, or good friends? Make sure you're up-to-date! For those who are not in a family relationship, and where this personal affirmation might not be understood, you can tell them, "Jesus loves you." Some people have never been told this personally, and your doing so may bring healing to them.

SECTION III / SESSION 15

CHAPTER 15

CONSECRATION

First, we must be saved—born again in Jesus Christ. After this we need to be baptized in the Holy Spirit, so that God's love and power can be released through us. This work of the Holy Spirit will be impeded, however, unless we take a third step, *consecration,* in which, having received everything that God has to give us, we offer ourselves to God.

Some are able to consecrate themselves at the time of their new birth in Christ, or soon after, but it seems for most, the Baptism in the Holy Spirit helps us feel the need for consecration, and also shows us more clearly the areas of our lives that need to be given over to the Lord.

Many expect a "free ride" to heaven, without any effort on their part. They expect God to take away bad habits and cure wrong behavior patterns without much cooperation from them. It is true, of course, that we can only offer God that which He has given us, but He has given us free will, to keep for ourselves, or to offer back to Him. God offers us heaven freely in this life, if we will freely give ourselves to Him. We must be His captives if we would be set free, for we can only be free in Him. There isn't any no-man's land. If we tried to be free outside of God, we would be enslaved by the enemy.

Consecration opens the way to *sanctification,* which is the work of God the Holy Spirit to make us more like Jesus. The blocks to sanctification are found mainly in the soul: our psychological nature—intellect, will, emotions. Here Satan gets in his strongest attacks, and here is where the Holy Spirit wants to work. If the soul is put in order, the spirit is free to rule the soul, and the soul to rule the body. The body with its normal physical drives is not the center of our problems. These drives are not bad in themselves, but are made evil and twisted by wrong attitudes in the soul, which produce wrong habit patterns in both soul and body.

Romans 6:6 says that "our old man was crucified with him . . . that . . . we might no longer be enslaved to sin" (RSV). The "old man" can't be the problem, since he *has been* crucified! No, it's the "flesh"—by which Paul means, not just the physical body, but the body corrupted by the earthbound and self-centered soul. It is the flesh, the self-life, and all it entails that must be "crucified," and not just once, but it must "die daily" in consecration in order that the real human being—spirit, soul, and body—can live unto God. Our spirit has been reborn, our soul is being sanctified, our body is being made whole now and is yet to be glorified. All these are part of the total salvation God is working out in us.

Questions for Your Home Study

1. What is consecration? _____

_____

_____

2. What are some other terms used for consecration?

_____

_____

3. Once we have made an initial act of consecration, will we ever need to renew it? _____

_____

_____

4. The unconsecrated believer makes Jesus go _____ where _____ wants to go, while the consecrated believer _____ Jesus where He _____

5. What do you think the Bible means by "deny yourself"? _____

_____

6. What scriptural understanding of the nature of man is of great importance to the gaining and maintaining of our consecration? _____

7. Salvation is primarily for the _____ of
    man; the Baptism in the Spirit is primarily for the
    _____ of man; consecration is primarily for the
    _____ of man, although   each is also for
    the whole person.

8. What part of man was particularly created to have
    fellowship with God? (Use the English and Greek
    words for your answer.)   _____
    _____

9. Write some Scriptures which show that the Father,
    Son, and the Holy Spirit live in the Christian's
    spirit.   _____
    _____
    _____
    _____

10. What part of man has ruled the unregenerated
    man's life since the fall? (Use English and Greek
    words.) What are its three parts?   _____
    _____
    _____

11. Explain sanctification.   _____
    _____
    _____

12. When does a person's body become the "temple of
    the Holy Spirit"? _____
    _____
    _____
    _____

13. Your spirit in union with the Holy Spirit is
    supposed to be the ruler of your _____
    and your submitted soul is supposed to direct your

    _____

14. Because the soul is a mixture of good and evil and
    a real battleground, does this mean that it is no
    good and that it is to be abolished? Why, or why
    not? Give Scripture. _____

    _____

    _____

15. What is the most difficult area of the soul to yield
    to the Holy Spirit? Why do you suppose this is true?

    _____

    _____

16. Define man's will. _____

    _____

    _____

17. Why is it wrong to depend upon emotions to guide
    your life? What happens to believers who do this?

    _____

    _____

18. Salvation brings a rest to the _____
    of man. The Baptism in the Spirit brings a rest to
    the _____ of the Christian.
    Maintaining this rest is greatly assisted by our
    learning to distinguish between the _____ and
    the _____ and thereby learning to
    walk in the _____

Large-Group Meeting

Prayer

Lord, we thank You for giving us absolutely everything we need! Please help us to give ourselves, souls and bodies to You, so that Your Spirit may flow out through us without being blocked by the tangles and snarls that our old life may have left in our souls. May the power of Your Spirit free us to express Jesus to the world more perfectly. We claim this in Jesus' name.

Scripture

"I beseech you therefore, brethren, by the mercies of God, that ye present your bodies a living sacrifice, holy, acceptable unto God, which is your reasonable service. And be not conformed to this world: but be ye transformed by the renewing of your mind, that ye may prove what is that good, and acceptable, and perfect, will of God." (Rom. 12 :1-2)

"And I pray God your whole spirit and soul and body be preserved blameless unto the coming of our Lord Jesus Christ." (I Thess. 5:23b)

Commentary

The leader will share from the Commentary found at the beginning of the chapter, and will add to it as he or she feels led.

Prayer and Praise

Suggested songs: "From Glory to Glory He's Changing Me," "Oh, to Be Like Thee!," "Thou Mighty Christ," (change last two phrases of this song to read: "Take

Thou my life and let it be Thy throne, Oh Lord, rule Thou in me."), "This Is My Rest Forever." After prayer and praise, break into small discussion groups.

Small-Group Discussion

1. What do you think Paul means when he speaks of consecration as our "reasonable service"? Look up various translations of this and talk about it.

2. Some believe that the "old man" is still alive, and that we are really made up of two people—the old man, and the new creature, which will continue to fight inside of us all our lives. Is this true? Give Scripture to support your answer. What effect would this belief have on your attitude toward the Christian's walk in the Spirit? What two parts of man *are* at odds *until* we learn submission to the Holy Spirit?

3. What can a Christian do to discipline his thought life? What should he do if unworthy thoughts enter his mind? Give helpful Scripture in this regard.

4. Why did God give man free will? Does He ever take it away? Why, or why not?

5. Have you ever tried to love someone without emotion? Is there a difference between emotion and emotionalism?

6. Is it wrong to want to be educated? Why is it that our colleges and universities today are such battlegrounds? Is the whole person being recognized in the curriculum of most institutions of higher education today?

7. Explain what happens to some Christians, even after the Baptism in the Holy Spirit, causing them to revert back to their old ways of acting and thinking temporarily and in some rare cases almost entirely.

8. Have you had any experiences in expressing God's love to others, or experiencing God's love yourself this week? Tell about it if you feel free to do so.

Conclusion

The whole group comes back together to share the fresh insights of the small groups. The cassette tape may be played. The meeting concludes with a further time of praise and prayer. Since we have been talking about consecration in depth, perhaps there are some who have never taken the initial step and would like to do it now. The leader should ask people to close their eyes to minimize self-consciousness and then ask those wanting to make an act of consecration to raise their hands. He can then lead them in a prayer of offering their bodies and souls to God.

Practical Application

Can you think of an instance when you chose to make the right decision, realizing that you were standing in the Spirit against your own self or soul's desires which were not God's absolute best for your life? Look for opportunities to do this again this week. Keep a record—perhaps on the note page at the end of this chapter—reminding you of what happened.

Look for opportunities for your spirit to rule your body's desires, for example, resisting the desire to overeat, or otherwise overindulge yourself. Other practical things are: getting enough exercise, getting to bed on time. These are all simple ways in which you can consecrate your body to the Lord. The Holy Spirit may move you to stronger disciplines, such as fasting. Keep track of these things, and be prepared to share them with the class.

NOTES

SECTION III / SESSION 16

CHAPTER 16

THE NARROW WAY

We have interpreted Jesus' teaching about the "narrow way" in terms of *accuracy* rather than *difficulty*. Jesus undoubtedly meant also to say that the way would prove difficult, for He tells us to "strive" to enter in at the narrow gate. But Jesus also said that His yoke was easy and His burden light, and that it is the Father's good pleasure to give us the kingdom (Matt. 11:30; Luke 12:32). We have tried to show in this chapter that it is not *God* who makes the narrow way difficult, but the enemy. Too many people avoid becoming Christians because they have the idea that the spiritual life is a hard, dull, struggling kind of thing. Thus they miss the unspeakable joys of fellowship with

God, and perhaps, alas, never find God at all. The idea that to be a Christian means to give up everything that is any "fun" in order to gain the doubtful privilege of going to a "heaven" that will really be a protracted "church service," is an idea that dies hard!

For this reason we have chosen to emphasize *accuracy* in speaking of the narrow way. It is important to see that we are not talking of compromises, or averages. We have explained that the way between two extremes isn't just a colorless compromise, but that once we find the narrow way, we can move ahead with a speed and ease that would not be possible if we got off the track. It is good to compare this "accuracy" with the word "righteousness." To be "righteous" is simply to be *right*, to be in tune with God and His ways. To be moving in the right way, the right place, the right time, the right relationship, the right speed.

A good illustration of the "narrow way" is the "window" which a spacecraft must pass through in order to enter orbit properly. This "window" is totally theoretical, and there is nothing to stop the spacecraft from occupying any other area of the heavens. There is no real window, with top, sides, etc., but there is a very limited, definite area through which the space ship must pass if it is going to orbit successfully. So the "narrow way" may be hard to find at first, for it is a matter of correct direction and right aiming, but once it is found, life begins to move with joy and power!

Questions for Your Home Study

1. What did Jesus mean when He said the way which leads to life is narrow? _____

_____

_____

2. How does the Christian check his course to make sure he's still on the narrow way? Can you think of methods of doing this other than those listed in this chapter? _____

_____

_____

3. Has the narrow way been planned to purposely make it hard and full of burdens and troubles? Who is it that tries to make the Christian's way difficult?

_____

_____

4. Name five devices Satan uses to try to deflect Christians from the true course. _____

_____

_____

_____

_____

5. What is the enemy's main power? How can we defeat it? _____

_____

_____

6. As in most things, in the walk in the Spirit, the true way lies between the _____

   _____

7. Why is it dangerous to join an exclusive group of believers, or to put yourself under the leadership of an exclusivist teacher, who claims to have a special corner on the truth? _____

   _____

   _____

   _____

8. What are some of the modern counterparts of the Judaizers in the New Testament? (p. 199) _____

   _____

   _____

   _____

9. a. What are some of the extremes through which the narrow way passes? Can you think of some to add to those given in this chapter? _____

   _____

   _____

   b. Is the narrow way just a compromise? If not, can you give some analogies of what it is supposed to be like? (p. 201) _____

   _____

   _____

10. The S _____
    and the W_____
    must always go together. _____

Large-Group Meeting

Prayer

Father, let us walk with Jesus on the path that leads to more and more life and joy, and finally brings us to You and Your home, which is our home, too. Help us to recognize the deflections of the enemy, so that we won't be turned aside or derailed, but let us keep our eyes on Your Son, and cultivate His presence in us, through Your Holy Spirit. Keep us on the narrow way by loving You so much that no other way has any appeal. Thank You, Father. In Jesus' name.

Scripture

"Enter ye in at the strait gate: for wide is the gate, and broad is the way, that leadeth to destruction, and many there be which go in thereat: Because strait is the gate, and narrow is the way, which leadeth unto life, and few there be that find it. Beware of false prophets, which come to you in sheep's clothing, but inwardly they are ravening wolves. Ye shall know them by their fruits. Do men gather grapes of thorns, or figs of thistles? Even so every good tree bringeth forth good fruit; but a corrupt tree bringeth forth evil fruit. A good tree cannot bring forth evil fruit, neither can a corrupt tree bring forth good fruit. Every tree that bringeth not forth good fruit is hewn down, and cast into the fire. Wherefore by their fruits ye shall know them." (Matt. 7:13-20)

Commentary

The leader will share from the Commentary found at the beginning of the chapter and will add to it as he or she feels led.

Prayer and Praise

Suggested songs: "His Yoke Is Easy," "Walking With the King," "I Must Have Jesus in My Whole Life," "Filled With God." Praise God for setting your feet on the right pathway and for correcting your course as needed! After a period of prayer and praise, break into small discussion groups.

Small-Group Discussion

1. When Jesus tells us to walk the narrow way, does this mean He wants us to be strait-laced and up-tight?

2. Does the word "narrow" sound appealing to the world? Why do you think this is?

3. Did Jesus promise that He would make the way hard and the burdens heavy? Why, or why not? Give Scriptures. Should we live in such a way as to convey this picture to others?

4. How do you answer the person who says something like, "Forty years ago I went to a 'Holy-Roller' meeting! Boy, no more of that for me!"

5. Do you need to be on the defensive if a person says to you, "I know someone who got involved in

this Pentecostal movement, and he ran off with another man's wife"? Why or why not?

6. How do you answer the person who says he is "rightly dividing the word of truth" when he cuts the Scripture up into "dispensations," and assigns certain parts of the New Testament to certain times of history? What if he says further that very little of it applies to the twentieth century, especially denying that the miracles and gifts of the Spirit apply to us today? (Some dispensationalists only have the Book of Ephesians left "for today"!)

7. There is a saying which goes something like this: "A broad stream is shallow; but a narrow stream runs deep." Can you think of a Scripture which explains that the understanding of the world is shallow when it comes to comprehending the things of God?

8. Was it easier to make the right decisions this week? Did you see any progress in changing old habit patterns for the better? Share something good that happened to you.

Conclusion

Large group resumes for sharing, tape, and praise.

Practical Application

Some Christians bring a habit of worry into their new lives. Often they wonder if they really *are* doing the right things and walking on the "King's Highway." If this applies

NOTES

to you, then ask yourself, "Has the Lord directed me in my present work, and does He give me satisfaction in it?" "Am I having fellowship with Him through praise and prayer and feeding on the Scripture?" "Am I trying to do what He tells me, and avoiding doing things that I know are wrong?" "Am I having spiritual fellowship with other believers?" If the answer to these questions is yes, then the Lord *must be* guiding your pathway! Faith means to trust Jesus. Are you trusting Him to love you enough to watch over you? Using your concordance, write down all the Scriptures you can find on God's guidance for His children. Read them daily for a while or make a tape recording and listen to them on the way to work or around the house. Thank Jesus daily that He is your Shepherd and is guiding you. By faith begin to thank Him right now!

Look in the mirror and see if you look like an up-tight Christian! Ask someone close to you to honestly tell you if you would fit into this category. Ask the Lord to show you how this way of thinking and acting can be changed. Write down what He shows you.

NOTES

SECTION III / SESSION 17

CHAPTER 17

THE CHARTS

We have compared the Christian's walk, the narrow way, to a navigational heading. Obviously, to follow a correct heading, we need a chart or map. That map is, first of all, the Bible, the Holy Scriptures of the Old and New Testaments. Secondly, it is theology, derived from the Bible, and from human experience tested by the Bible. Thirdly, it is helpful books written by wise fellow-Christians, commenting on the Scriptures, and on the theology derived from the Scriptures. Finally, each church or tradition has something to contribute to all this from its own background and experience.

There are a lot of things written on any chart that do not apply to the person using it. Some of the information on a chart you may never find applicable to your particular needs, but you don't tear up or ignore the chart for that reason. The part you use is that which applies to your journey in your particular vessel. It's the same with Scripture. There is much in the Bible you may not understand, that you may not feel you will ever understand. There is much that does not apply to you and your journey, although you cannot say that it *will never* apply. Don't be put off by the parts that you don't understand. Let the Holy Spirit show you what applies to you.

We have said that you will get in trouble by trying to have experience without truth, or the Spirit without the Word. Don't forget that the opposite is even more dangerous: the Word without the Spirit; truth without experience. Paul says of this: "The letter killeth," then adds "but the Spirit giveth life." This describes the Bible without the Holy Spirit to illuminate it. Let the Spirit light up the Scripture for you and lead you through its pages.

Questions for Your Home Study

1. What is the "chart" for Christians?_____

_____

2. In order to be able to understand the Bible, which do you think would be the most helpful? (Underline the correct answer.)
   a. to be able to read it in the original Hebrew and Greek.

b. to have received Jesus and to have been baptized in the Spirit.

3. What is the minimum amount of Scripture we should try to read daily? _____

_____

_____

4. If a new Christian decides to read the Bible through, what order of reading would you suggest for him?

_____

_____

_____

5. What are proof texts? How can they be misleading?

_____

_____

6. How can we be prepared to answer the person who quotes proof texts out of context to confirm a doctrine? _____

_____

_____

7. The most important ministry of the Bible to the unbeliever is to witness to _____

_____

8. The most important ministry of the Bible to the believer is to bring _____
This means that _____ is speaking to us personally through _____

9. The Christian life must be an interplay of _____
   _____ and _____
   What does this mean? _____
   _____
   _____

10. If you find something you don't understand or don't
    like in the Bible, what should you do about it? ___
    _____
    _____

11. "Mark" the Scriptures really means we should ___
    _____
    them, but it also can mean that we should _____
    _____ the words that especially
    speak to us.

12. Why should we memorize Scripture? _____
    _____
    _____

13. What does it mean to "inwardly digest" the
    Scriptures? Why is this important? _____
    _____
    _____

14. What is theology? Why is it needed? _____
    _____
    _____
    _____

15. What are the best-known brief summaries of theology? Why did these originally come into existence? _____

_____

_____

_____

_____

16. In the light of Christian history, what does the Scripture mean: "Submit yourselves one to another in the fear of God"? _____

_____

_____

_____

17. Why should you respect your pastor, even though you don't agree with him, or he with you, in certain areas? _____

_____

_____

_____

Large-Group Meeting

Prayer

Thank You for the Scriptures, Father, and help us to use them properly. May we be able to recognize right teaching, and rightly teach others, so that those who don't know Jesus can come to know Him, and those who know Him, may come to know Him better. In Jesus' name.

Scripture

"And that from a child thou hast known the holy scriptures, which are able to make thee wise unto salvation through faith which is in Christ Jesus. All scripture is given by inspiration of God, and is profitable for doctrine, for reproof, for correction, for instruction in righteousness: That the man of God may be perfect, thoroughly furnished unto all good works." (II Tim. 3:15-17)

Commentary

The leader will share from the Commentary found at the beginning of the chapter, and will add to it as he or she feels led.

Prayer and Praise

Suggested songs: "All Over the World," (add verses, such as: "All over my church, the Spirit is moving," "All over *Seattle*" [name your city], "All over this room," etc.), "Make Mention That His Name Is Exalted," "The Day of Thy Power." Some time might be spent in letting those so led share a favorite Scripture verse either from memory or by reading it.

Small-Group Discussion

1. Share your favorite translation or paraphrase of the Scriptures. Compare it with the King James Version; give pros and cons on both.

2. What plan of daily Bible reading have you found to be the most helpful?

3. What is the difference between proof-text Bible study and topical Bible study?

4. What are some books that have helped you most with Bible study?

5. Give an example of a verse or passage from the Scripture that has spoken to you individually— similar to the example of J. A. Dennis in the book.

6. Can the Holy Spirit inspire you with a Biblical reference you have never read or learned? Share your experience on this. Has anyone in the group ever been given "chapter and verse" by the Holy Spirit?

7. Tell about the type of Bible-study class which has been most meaningful in your understanding the Scriptures and in making real, positive changes in your personal life. (You may want to leave out the names of individual teachers or churches so that your answer will not seem competitive with others.)

8. What method have you found helpful in memorizing Scriptures?

9. If you are familiar with one or more of the Creeds or Confessions, tell if and why it is meaningful to you.

10. What other books have you found beneficial in assisting you to understand your faith?

11. What "treasure" does your denomination have to share with all Christians?

12. If any member of the group knows another language, let him share insights that have come to him from reading the Bible in that language.

13. Share some of the encouraging Scriptures you found this week on the subject of God's guidance for His children, and any special help God gave you in guidance recently.

Conclusion

The whole group meets together again to share the insights from the smaller groups. The cassette tapes may be used at this time. The meeting concludes with a further period of praise and prayer. If anyone receives a special Scripture from the Lord they feel is for the group, they may be encouraged to share it spontaneously during the time of praise.

Practical Application

How does your time reading the Bible compare with the time spent reading other material: the latest magazine, the newspaper, the latest novel, etc.? How does it compare with the time spent watching TV? If you have not set yourself a plan of regular Bible reading, get started on it this week. Get started on memorizing, too, if you haven't done so. See below.

To husbands: As the head of your house, under Jesus, you should be guiding your family in daily Bible reading and prayer. If you are having difficulty with this, why not talk it over with your pastor or some other leader? It needs to be an interesting time that the family will look forward to.

To wives: If your husband is not a Christian, you should tactfully try to establish some kind of daily Bible reading and prayer under your own direction, for your children. You must do this without being offensive to your husband, or seeming to usurp the headship, which is still his, even though he is not yet a believer. This will require some Godgiven wisdom on your part, and much love. When your husband comes to Christ, be ready to step back as quickly as possible and let him take his rightful 'place in leading the family Bible reading and prayer. If you are raising a family without a father in the home, you will of course be carrying out the leadership yourself in these things.

Hints on Memorizing

You will find much benefit in memorizing, not just isolated texts from the Scripture, but whole passages and chapters. The task is not as formidable as you might think. In the first place, if you have been a churchgoer at all, you undoubtedly have more of the Bible in your memory than you realize, just from hearing it read or quoted, or from your Sunday-school days. Next, you don't have to consciously retain everything you memorize. If you memorize a passage one week, and two weeks later you can't recite it completely and accurately, that doesn't mean it's lost to you. Your mind has retained it, but you are not able completely to recall it. Don't worry! The Holy Spirit will bring it to mind when He needs to, but you have put it into your memory bank.

One helpful technique for memorizing is to take a chapter or passage and cover the opening words with a three-by-five file card. Try to say the opening words of the passage, then move the card down to check yourself. Try the next phrase, still covered by the card, and again check yourself. If you can't get started on the next phrase, move the card just enough to give yourself a clue, and see how far you can go. Another good system for taking advantage of time that would be otherwise unusable for memorizing is to get a small tape recorder and record the passage you are working on, leaving space between phrases; then, when you are driving somewhere, or working around the house, turn the machine on, and first repeat the phrases following the tape, then try to say the phrases *before* the recorder plays them. You will be surprised how quickly you will learn. These are just two suggestions. Each will have his or her own best way to do it, but be sure that you do memorize.

NOTES

CHAPTER 18

THE COMPASS

In this closing chapter of the book, we are talking about how to live as Christians in an unbelieving world, keeping ourselves sensitized to the Holy Spirit. It is very hard to walk in the Spirit when you are out in the world, and sometimes the most difficult place is in your own family! You need to learn how to let the love and power of God flow out from you to the world in which you live, without letting the darkness and evil of the world flow back in and quench your new life. The main way to do this is by keeping the outflow of God's life constant and strong, and this in turn will come about when fellowship with Him is unclouded.

We must always keep the channels open between us and God, first of all by praise, then by prayer—both of these with the mind and with the Spirit—in our own language, and in tongues. We must confess our sins and faults right away, and receive God's forgiveness. We must see to it that we confess to others when we have wronged them, and make restitution as much as is in our power to do. We must forgive those who have wronged us. We need to consecrate ourselves to God, and we need to reconsecrate ourselves many times in the day.

We must be careful of our recreation, entertainment, and manner of life, not only for the example we set to others, but because of the effect on our own life in the Spirit. We need fellowship with others in the Spirit, and we must be thoughtful in selecting this fellowship, avoiding the "exclusivists" of any sort. We must seek opportunity to tell others about Jesus (and this is one of the greatest stimulants to the life of the Spirit in us). We must not be afraid to let the gifts of the Spirit flow through us to others, so that God can minister to them in their needs, and also to emphasize the reality of our witness.

We must be openhanded and ready to share with others the material blessings God has given us. Our finances, too, must be consecrated to God. He can bless us as we bless others. We must "deal our bread to the hungry"; we must be concerned, as God directs us, about the needs of the people in the world around us. We cannot withdraw from the society in which we live. We must neither join the kind of "social activists" who go out to heal the world's ills, but forget or disbelieve in the power of God, nor must we be found with the "ivory tower" type of Christians who try to ignore the needs of the world and only "live in the glory."

Questions for Your Home Study

1. Is the "compass" of the Christian the Holy Spirit? If not, what is it? ⎯⎯⎯⎯⎯⎯⎯⎯⎯⎯⎯

    ⎯⎯⎯⎯⎯⎯⎯⎯⎯⎯⎯⎯⎯⎯⎯⎯⎯⎯⎯⎯

2. What does it mean to "sensitize" our compasses, and how do we do it?⎯⎯⎯⎯⎯⎯⎯⎯⎯⎯

    ⎯⎯⎯⎯⎯⎯⎯⎯⎯⎯⎯⎯⎯⎯⎯⎯⎯⎯⎯⎯

    ⎯⎯⎯⎯⎯⎯⎯⎯⎯⎯⎯⎯⎯⎯⎯⎯⎯⎯⎯⎯

3. What does it really mean to "serve the Lord"?⎯⎯

    ⎯⎯⎯⎯⎯⎯⎯⎯⎯⎯⎯⎯⎯⎯⎯⎯⎯⎯⎯⎯

    ⎯⎯⎯⎯⎯⎯⎯⎯⎯⎯⎯⎯⎯⎯⎯⎯⎯⎯⎯⎯

4. Why did God create mankind? ⎯⎯⎯⎯⎯⎯⎯⎯

    ⎯⎯⎯⎯⎯⎯⎯⎯⎯⎯⎯⎯⎯⎯⎯⎯⎯⎯⎯⎯

    ⎯⎯⎯⎯⎯⎯⎯⎯⎯⎯⎯⎯⎯⎯⎯⎯⎯⎯⎯⎯

5. What are some of the things you should do during your daily devotions? ⎯⎯⎯⎯⎯⎯⎯⎯⎯

    ⎯⎯⎯⎯⎯⎯⎯⎯⎯⎯⎯⎯⎯⎯⎯⎯⎯⎯⎯⎯

    ⎯⎯⎯⎯⎯⎯⎯⎯⎯⎯⎯⎯⎯⎯⎯⎯⎯⎯⎯⎯

6. Explain the difference between thanks and praise.

    ⎯⎯⎯⎯⎯⎯⎯⎯⎯⎯⎯⎯⎯⎯⎯⎯⎯⎯⎯⎯

    ⎯⎯⎯⎯⎯⎯⎯⎯⎯⎯⎯⎯⎯⎯⎯⎯⎯⎯⎯⎯

    ⎯⎯⎯⎯⎯⎯⎯⎯⎯⎯⎯⎯⎯⎯⎯⎯⎯⎯⎯⎯

7.   Should we ask God for things, or is this selfish?
Give Scripture for your answer_____
_____
_____

8.   If you don't know how to pray in a particular
situation, what should you do? _____
_____
_____

9.   What is the greatest sin, and how can this apply to
Christians who already have received Jesus? _____
_____
_____

10. If you are in a church where there is no spiritual
activity that really feeds you, what should you do?
_____
_____
_____

11. What is a most important thing to look for when
selecting a church or prayer group for fellowship
or when selecting a teacher? _____
_____
_____

12. When is the only time a Christian should separate
himself from others? _____
_____
_____

13. When do you become a member of the church? ___

_____

_____

14. What is the most vulnerable kind of Christian?___

_____

_____

15. Give some pointers on making an effective witness
    about Jesus Christ. _____

_____

_____

16. Are the gifts of the Holy Spirit helpful when
    witnessing? How can they be? _____

_____

17. All that the Christian has belongs to God, but much
    of this God desires us to use for the support of our
    own family, and for our own maintenance. What
    would be a good way to decide how much of our
    substance should be shared with others? What is
    the scriptural standard? _____

_____

_____

_____

_____

18. Explain the difference between tithes and offerings.

_____

_____

19. What are some of the areas of recreation and entertainment that Christians should be cautious about? _____

_____

_____

_____

20. What is the relationship of social action—that is, good deeds done in society—to the Christian life? Is it important for a believer to be doing good works for others? Did Jesus just tell us to be good to other *believers?* Give Scripture. _____

_____

_____

_____

21. Although Jesus didn't write a book, or travel very far from his birthplace, yet He had a plan to reach the ends of the earth with His message and love. What was this plan? _____

_____

Large-Group Meeting

Prayer

"Direct us, O Lord, in all our doings, with Thy most gracious favor, and further us with continual help; that in all our works begun, continued, and ended in Thee, we may glorify Thy Holy Name . . . through Jesus Christ our Lord. Amen." *(The Book of Common Prayer)*

Scripture

"Now what use is it, my brothers, for a man to say he
"has faith' if his actions do not correspond with it? Could
that sort of faith save anyone's soul? If a fellow man or
woman has no clothes to wear and nothing to eat, and one
of you say, 'Good luck to you, I hope you'll keep warm
and find enough to eat,' and yet give them nothing to meet
their physical needs, what on earth is the good of that? Yet
that is exactly what a bare faith without a corresponding
life is like—useless and dead. . . . Faith without action is
as dead as a body without a soul." (James 2:14-17, 26
Phillips)

Commentary

The leader will share from the Commentary found at
the beginning of the chapter and will add to it as he or she
feels led.

Summary

Just as wars are won, in spite of airplanes and other
devices of modern combat, by ground troops occupying
territory, so the war against the enemy of our souls will be
won by individual people telling other individual people
about Jesus, meeting their needs in the power and love of
God, leading them to a saving faith in Jesus, and to the
fullness of the Holy Spirit and the receiving of His power.
Books, lectures, meetings, tape recordings, etc., are all

important helps, but in the last analysis, victory in the world depends on you, telling others the *full* Gospel, the good news of Jesus.

Prayer and Praise

Suggested songs: "Thou Art Worthy!," "I Will Bless the Lord at All Times," "The Lord Hath Done Great Things," "I Will Praise Him," (for a second verse, sing "Glory, glory to the Father, Glory, glory to the Son, Glory, glory to the Spirit, Glory to the Three in One," and then repeat first verse). After a time of praise and singing, with your understanding and in the Spirit, break into smaller groups for discussion.

Small-Group Discussion

1. Which do you think would be the best: parents who make a blanket condemnation of movies, television, popular music, etc., or parents who help their children to know which movie, television show, or popular songs they should or shouldn't participate in? Which group of children would be best prepared for life away from home?

2. Is it important for a Christian to pay his bills? What should he do if he can't?

3. How should a Christian employer treat his employees? Find some Scripture on this if you can.

4. How should a Christian employee treat his employer? Scripture reference?

5. Discuss effective ways to keep your family from depending too much on commercial entertainment.

6. What are ways in which your family can help others?

7. Should believers be concerned with "social action," that is, working for fair dealing in business and society? What would be the right or wrong way to go about this?

8. If a person tells two others about Jesus, and leads them to accept Him, and to receive the power of the Holy Spirit, and they in turn the next day each tell two others, lead them to the Lord, and to the Baptism in the Holy Spirit, and this pattern continues—each person telling two others each day—in twenty-nine days, less than a single month, some 250 million people would have been reached, more than the entire population of the United States! In just a few more days, the number would equal the population figure for the whole world! * "But they wouldn't all listen!" you may say. True, but millions would. Why doesn't something like this happen? Would it be likely to happen unless people were being baptized in the Holy Spirit? Why, or why not? Since millions have been baptized in the Spirit, why isn't it happening in greater numbers? What can we do to help this kind of witness become a reality?

Conclusion

The entire group meets together, and shares the insights that have come from the small group sessions. The cassette tape may be played. The meeting ends with a further period of prayer and praise. By now there should be great unity in the group, and considerable freedom in prayer and praise. Hopefully, you will want to stay together for further study and fellowship.

Practical Application

Think about your personal life: manners, house, office, care of children, care of your property, clothing, etc. Ask yourself: "How would it appear to me, if I were observing all this? Would these things help the witness to Christ or detract from it? You may want to discuss these things with your wife or husband, or with a close friend to get a clearer viewpoint.

---

* For the mathematically minded: Check our figures on page 223 in *The Holy Spirit and You*. Is there a mistake? If so, will you please correct it for us!

Footnotes

1. The 1973 Encyclopedia Britannica stated, "When, in, 1960, Father Dennis Bennett announced to his congregation, St. Mark's Episcopal at Van Nuys, CA, that he experienced a new out pouring of God's Spirit, the recent [charismatic] movement can be said to have begun."

2. Though the Rev. Bennett died November 1, 1991 on "All Saints Day," his work is carried on through his widow, Rita Bennett. She continues the work they co-founded at Christian Renewal Association, Inc., Edmonds, Washington in 1968.

3. Holy Spirit and You audiotapes or CD-rom disks are available. There are a total of 18 thirty- minute lessons which match the 18 chapters. Dennis and Rita Bennett are the teachers of this additional teaching material. You will enjoy having fellowship with them and gaining further spiritual insights.

4. Again you may use the 30 minute audio tape or CD-rom here to enrich your class. This message will not be repeated in further chapters.

Other books by Dennis and Rita Bennett:

The Holy Spirit and You
The Trinity of Man

by Dennis Bennett:

How To Pray for the Release of the Holy Spirit
Nine O'Clock in the Morning